FROM STILETTOS TO THE STOCK EXCHANGE

Inside the Life of a Serial Entrepreneur

By Tina Aldatz

FROM STILETTOS TO THE STOCK EXCHANGE

Helen's
CONTINENTAL
BEAUTY SALON

(Former Sorg Beauty Salon)

13 E. Merchant St.   New Buffalo   Ph: 469-0056

Winner of several International Hairdresser
Competitions & Gold Trophy Awards

Our Permanents,
Color & High Styles
Are Long Lasting

OPERATORS:
Phyllis Aldatz, Alena Odstrcilek, Lauretta Abele
& Helen Snajdr

Also Operating Our Salon In Union Pier
Phone 469-4423

Campus hair stylest

Published by Apparel Insiders LLC

Cover Art by Tracie Taylor

Layout and design by Sundree Branding

TinaAldatz.com

Printed in the U.S.A.

This is a work of creative nonfiction. The events and details
are portrayed to the best of Tina Aldatz's memory. While all the
stories in this book are true, some names and identifying details
have been changed to protect the privacy of the people involved.

I dedicate this book in loving memory to my aunt, Angela (Tia Lonnie) Rodriguez.

ACKNOWLEDGMENTS

I want to first thank my mother and father for giving me life; my family for their love and support over the years; my grandfather Jesus Cesar Aldatz for literally teaching me how to take my first steps in life; and my grandmother Josefina Diaz Aldatz for migrating from Mexico to America in the 1920s. Without her, I would not be here today as a successful Latina-American woman.

I thank the families who allowed me to become a "Lee Press-On ® Kid," a knack I developed as a pre-teen of "sticking" onto families I considered normal in the same way the popular brand of nails would to a woman's fingernails: the Wagners, the Renshaws, the Eaves, the Vosses, the Smidts, the Curries, and the Elmores. Your kindness, generosity and willingness to share your homes, traditions and love will forever be in my heart. To the Good Shepherd Shelter for battered women in Los Angeles: thank you for taking us in when we hit rock bottom.

To my brother Rocky a.k.a "Joe Positive" for always being my personal coach and lifting my spirits or bringing me back to reality when I needed him most and for the gift of being an auntie to my nephew Ky. To my sister Angela for the amazing song list in this book, for being the keeper of our family's memories and for the gift of being an Auntie to my niece Jaz. To my brother Richard, thank you for giving me two beautiful nephews. To my sister Kady for being the "Gestapo" when I go on shopping sprees (hee hee) and to our baby brother Eric, who is the closest I will ever be to having a son; I am so proud of you Mijo.

I thank Holly Davis for allowing me to be a mother figure to my siblings, by far my greatest challenge and accomplishment.

To my best friend and soul sister Margarita Rosa de Temple Floris for saving my ass so many times, being my rock (and roll), and the greatest influence in my life as a business partner, friend, and funniest, fucking coolest chick I know...por vida!

I thank the University of California Irvine Burn Center for taking care of me after I suffered 3rd degree burns to the soles of my feet. God bless the doctors and nurses in this world!

Thank you to DeAnna L. Carpenter for helping me get my words on paper and to Tracie Taylor for her vision and excellent photography. I appreciate you both for helping me express and capture my message.

I'd like to give a special thanks to Mr. Michael Atmore of Footwear News for literally "getting my foot in the door." Without your generosity and support, *Foot Petals Inc.* might not have happened.

Finally, to RG Barry Corporation for believing in *Foot Petals Inc.* and allowing the brand to continue to grow far beyond the "Tina & Margie Show."

FORWARD

"WHAT IS A CHRYSALIS?"

Tina Aldatz's *From Stilettos to the Stock Exchange* is a primer on the four life stages of her metamorphosis from teen and early entrepreneur, from a young LA to a young New York executive, to a creator of a business that would be sold for millions, to today's mature philanthropist. She's committed time and money to the cause of bringing self-sufficiency to low income women coming from backgrounds just like hers. Her objective in this book was to share her life's trials and tribulations, her dreams and her ambitions, her failures and her successes, and ultimately the secrets to her success. If you close your eyes after reading each word, page, and chapter you will hear the melody of a bittersweet saga of rags to riches. Tina simply provides the lyrics.

The title *From Stilettos to the Stock Exchange* says it all as Tina's journey takes you from the tough streets of Los Angeles to the hallowed halls of the New York Stock Exchange. Not only were her stiletto's part of her uniform, but the misery that they so many times caused her, ended up leading to the spark of an idea that would yield millions.

Tina's ambition, tenacity, good heart, charitable nature, and deadeye focus are traits that served as a chrysalis of the hard shell around her. The kind hard case that protects a caterpillar as it goes through the phases of metamorphosis before emerging as a butterfly, her chrysalis protected her as she faced impossible odds, grappled with a dysfunctional family environment, endured financial losses, and survived personal losses of loved ones. Her combination of simple talk and able story telling will convince you that no matter what obstacles you face in life, happiness and success can be yours if you follow your dreams and stay the course no matter what barriers block your way.

I will keep several copies of Tina's book in my office. They will serve as gifts to anyone I meet that thinks achieving success is not in their DNA.

Jim Issler
President, Chief Executive Officer
H.H. Brown

PAYING IT FORWARD

I am often asked how I define "success." My answer each time is that I define my success by the success of those whom I have been privileged to pay it forward to. I've found that paying it forward doesn't necessarily have to be monetary; it can be a random act of kindness, a simple thank you, or giving someone that "shot" regardless of his/her experience or credentials.

In my career, from my job as a receptionist at *Parnelli Jones* to eventually starting *Foot Petals*, I have been given many "shots" and have been the beneficiary of countless people's decision to pay it forward. I am especially grateful for the opportunities and resources that have afforded me the chance to pay it forward through organizations such as Girls Incorporated of Orange County, Two Ten Foundation's Women In the Footwear Industry (WIFI) and the Hispanic 100 Foundation. Thank you for allowing me to lead the Hispanic 100 Mentor Program. I am committed to keeping the kindness going and have designated an organization, and cause, close to my heart to benefit from the proceeds of this book.

A percentage of the sales of *From Stilettos to the Stock Exchange* will benefit the Two Ten Footwear Foundation's Women In the Footwear Industry (WIFI) program. The Two Ten Footwear Foundation has a 50+ year tradition of providing financial assistance, emotional support, and community resources to members of the footwear community in need.

It is my hope that the proceeds from this book will aid Two Ten's WIFI in paying it forward for innumerable footwear professionals and their families. You can learn more about this organization in the following pages.

ABOUT TWO TEN FOOTWEAR FOUNDATION

Two Ten Footwear Foundation changes the lives of people in the footwear community.

Deeply rooted in community, Two Ten Footwear Foundation began as an informal system of support between "shoe workers" during the Great Depression. Many had fallen on hard times due to loss of their jobs and were supported by their colleagues who literally passed a hat amongst themselves to collect money for those who were out of work. This highly personal outreach represented a unique unity within a trade that believed helping each other was as much about individual survival as it was health of an entire industry.

Realizing that passing a hat was not a sustainable way to provide financial assistance to their community, the group created a more organized effort that would lay the groundwork for its future. A modest cash donation and some office space at 210 Lincoln Street in industry-centric Boston, Massachusetts launched what became known as The Two Ten Associates, and the first formal, organized fund-raising efforts were launched including the first annual golf outing and annual dinner events.

75 years after its humble beginnings, Two Ten Footwear Foundation now serves an industry of over 250,000 footwear employees and their families through programs and services that directly impact their lives. Funded entirely through the generosity of the footwear community and Foundation partners, Two Ten's services include emergency financial assistance, scholarships and professional development, crisis counseling, career services, national networking events and much more. As the only philanthropy in the U.S. that focuses solely on supporting its own industry, Two Ten's legacy mission is clear: *to bring shoepeople together to help each other during crisis, support each other as a community, and ensure the future of the footwear industry.*

Building a footwear community has been one of Two Ten's key priorities from the very beginning. Today, the Foundation offers four targeted networking groups for the footwear community and its allied industries including Women in Footwear Industry (WIFI), Young Professionals for 210, Human Resources Leadership Committee and Footwear Cares®, a national month of community service.

Over the past few years, emergency calls for assistance placed to Two Ten have increased by 155% – of which, a staggering 70% are from women. WIFI recognizes the unique challenges facing women in the footwear industry. A national network, WIFI connects footwear women, supports their personal and professional growth and harnesses their talents and expertise to address socio-economic issues of concern to their colleagues, our industry and Two Ten Footwear Foundation.

To learn more about Two Ten's mission, its rich history and its offerings to the footwear community, visit www.twoten.org.

CONTENTS

"My Angels" from left: Armando, me and Lourdes DuPont

INTRODUCTION

Ding. Ding. The elevator doors opened. I stepped in and hit the button for the 20th floor taking a deep breath and smiling to mask my nervous excitement. As the elevator ascended, I looked over to Armando and Margie, a deep wave of gratitude sweeping over me. Just 10 years earlier, Armando had listened to me pitch my idea for a women's designer insole. I had no idea what I was doing and met with him to get some feedback on my presentation and business plan for potential investors. Margie, my best friend and business partner, came on board when my company was in its nascent stages, when the only product I had was a self-made prototype of a foot cushion. I didn't have the formal education, let alone the business savvy that would qualify me to even create a product, or start a business for that matter. I did, however, have passion and enthusiasm for what I wanted to do. I wholeheartedly believed in myself and my ability to create a product that would benefit countless others. Back then, I was hungry, literally and figuratively. I was unemployed and one of the main providers for my family. I had given myself half a year to create something big, something that would place me in a better financial position to take care of myself and my family. I had lost and experienced so much throughout my life that I figured I had nothing more to lose. I had no idea when I went into that meeting with Armando that I would leave it with him as my investor, but I did. There we were, 10 years later, headed to a meeting that neither of us could have foreseen. I was grateful that Armando and Margie would experience this with me. I was even more grateful that they had taken the chance on me and my dream; their belief and investment in my dream was a part of why we were even in that elevator in the first place.

We stepped into the hallway and were immediately greeted by several lawyers. "Good day

Ms. Aldatz; good day Mr. Dupont and Mrs. Floris," they said as they shook our hands and escorted us down a long hallway. I felt like Manny Pacquiao or Oscar de la Hoya headed into the boxing ring for a match with an entourage around me: It was time to get down to business and the day wouldn't be over until it was over. We walked into a well-lit, spacious meeting room with a rectangular oak conference table in the middle of the room. The table was long enough to seat at least 20 people. I scanned the table. There were at least 10 piles of paper, stacked about one-foot high or that's what it looked like to me, waiting for our signatures. The lawyers explained the paperwork before us as Armando and I sat down to start the process: *Foot Petals* – the $10 million in annual sales foot and shoe accessories company that I started in 2001 with an initial $10,000 investment from Armando – was being sold to R.G. Barry Corporation that day. I took out my pen and reached for the first stack of papers. It was going to be a long morning.

By noon, we had signed all but two stacks of forms. We continued to work through each stack, reading each word carefully and paying attention to the details. We were so entrenched in paperwork that the receptionist ordered lunch for us. As the last stack of papers was signed, the lawyers – who were on the phone the entire time verifying each form as we signed them – notified us that the wire transfer was about to begin. There was a computer already logged on and it would be a matter of minutes before the funds showed up in my account. I massaged my hands as I had a slight cramp from writing and engaged in small talk with the lawyers as we waited. Armando, Margie, and I shared in a few laughs as we reminisced on our journey together. We were happy and I could tell that they were just as excited as I was for what was happening. I was given the word that the transfer had completed, and stared at the computer in amazement as I received verification that $14 million was in my account. I clasped my hands then leaned over to hug Armando.

I sat there in a daze with the biggest smile plastered on my face, daydreaming of all the things I could do with $14 million. I considered a move to a remote island where I could live out the rest of my years surrounded by beauty and solitude. I snapped out of my daydream once I remembered that I had to transfer funds to all of my business partners. I had to divide the money among four parties: five percent to Armando, five percent to Margie, and 55 percent to the five Remington factory owners. The remaining 35 percent stayed in my account, as I was the single largest shareholder. As soon as the disbursements were made to each of my partners, the receptionist poured glasses of champagne. We toasted to a successful acquisition and I made my rounds with each of the lawyers. I left the conference room satisfied and optimistic about what was in store. On January 28, 2011, I had become a multi-millionaire.

I have always heard that a person's struggles would come either early in their life, in the middle of their life, or towards the end of their life. I'm thankful that my struggles came early in life. This was made abundantly clear as early as fourth grade when I saw one of my classmates picked up in a limousine. I wondered what made him so different and I became determined that my family and I would have access to the same things he did. I realized that there was more for

Me, now 2014 in front of my elementary school

me and that I didn't have to be a product of my circumstances and environment. I had my heart and mind set on being the best that I could be for myself and my family. My family has always been at the center of everything I've done and is the motivation for me to continue to be my best self. I cannot imagine being the woman I am today if even the smallest detail of my journey thus far was changed, deleted, or altered out of my life's story. Everything happened (and continues to happen) for a reason. Despite how challenging, painful, or embarrassing it might have been, I know that I am all the better because of it. I didn't know that an accident on the beach that left the soles of my feet with third-degree burns would, decades later, be the impetus and inspiration for the insole products I would create. There is never really a way to know what moments in our lives will go on to become major, life-changing influences. I've learned that rather than to judge and be ashamed of those moments, to be open to and embrace the possibilities that may come as a result of them. My life reflects this very thing.

I have toyed with the idea of writing a book for some years now, but struggled with fully committing to writing my story as it meant I'd have to share the good, the bad, and the unsavory parts that are easier to keep tucked away. I often speak with a lot of students, women, and aspiring entrepreneurs and one thing that remains consistent is that most people only see the finished product. They hardly ever consider the process that an individual had to go through to get to the finished product. I wasn't born into a wealthy family, I didn't hit the lottery, and I didn't finish high school. Like many people, the odds were stacked against me. I could've easily followed the

From left: Richard, Kady, Rocky, Eric, Angela and Tina.

Clockwise from top left: Rocky, Eric, Richard, Kady, Tina and Angela.

gang and drug lifestyle that I saw in my childhood and adolescent years, but I didn't. I knew that there was something more, something different for me and I followed that feeling. I had faith and believed that God would provide a way for me; and He did. I truly believe that anyone with a vision, a desire, and a willingness to work and learn along the way can do what I've done, and more. It takes work. Indeed it takes a lot of work. Like the adage goes: "Anything worth having is worth working for." Your dreams, goals, heart's desires, and ideas are no different.

I think a groundbreaking moment for me came once I realized how rich I was before becoming a multimillionaire. I had a family whom I loved and cherished, and who loved and cherished me in return. I had friends and mentors who believed in me and actively supported me in whatever capacity I needed them. And, I had a dream that gave me back everything that I put into it, and then some. That is true wealth; I believe that through acknowledging these things and being grateful for them, we make room to receive even more. Life does start with your perception.

Though you may not drive a great big Cadillac
Gansta whitewalls, TV antenna in the back
You many not drive a car at all,
but remember brothers and sisters
You can still stand tall
~ excerpt from Be Thankful For What You Got by William DeVaughn

My Cousin Johnny, Art Leboe and me

It is my hope that the following pages will inspire any and every person reading this book to believe in the power of their dreams. I cannot express enough how one must not be deterred by the hand life deals them, as even the most unpromising spread still has the potential of winning

I cannot express enough how one must not be deterred by the hand life deals them, as even the most unpromising spread still has the potential of winning the game if it is played right.

the game if it is played right. I share a lot of background on my childhood and adolescent years, as well as my early adult years up until the present to give you a glimpse into who I am as a person: my thoughts, my fears, and my joys. I also share the story of how *Foot Petals* came to be, my six essentials for business: The Three M's or best practices (Money, Marketing, and Management) and The Three R's or core values (Reputation, Resourcefulness, and Resilience) that I have found helpful along my path.

You'll find lyrics to songs strategically placed throughout as music was such a big part of my family and experiences growing up. There was always music playing in my household, and I like to think that if my life were a soundtrack, it'd include some of the greatest songs and "oldies" ever produced. Growing up, my parents would always listen to one of the greatest disc jockeys in Los Angeles, Art Laboe. I recently met him and he signed my dad's original KRLA bumper sticker from the 1970s. I was beyond stoked because I knew it would mean the world to my parents. Music helped me remain optimistic on my dark days and kept me glowing on my sunny days, so it goes without saying that I'd find a way to include music in this book. I must apologize in advance as I do cuss from time to time, but we managed to edit out a lot of those words. Hopefully you don't flinch too much if you see a profane word here and there. Lastly, I hope that in these pages you will find your reflection wrapped somewhere in the words, and be inspired to create and live the life you desire for yourself. I have heard it said that it is lonely at the top and as someone who has 'made it' I can say that the statement has some merit. It may be lonely at the top, but there's room for anyone with the drive and tenacity to see their dreams through. I believe that you can do it and I hope you believe that you can, too.

FROM STILETTOS TO THE STOCK EXCHANGE

Inside the Life of a Serial Entrepreneur

Me at 25 years old in front of Victoria's Secret, Madison and 57th Street, NYC

CHAPTER ONE

Follow the Passion, Follow the Fashion

There I was, 25 years old, plowing my way through the crowded and congested sidewalks of New York City. I was headed to my first day of work at Victoria's Secret in Manhattan, feeling accomplished and confident, having recently made the move from southern California where I worked as a co-manager with Victoria's Secret in a high-end Orange County mall. I had tried, to no avail, to work at Nordstrom's, which was my dream job. My friends were able to secure a job with the company, but for some strange reason, it didn't work for me. In Orange County I attended a training that further piqued my interest and curiosity in the company and fashion in general. Victoria's Secret was looking to extend its brand beyond lacy lingerie and was preparing to introduce a line of lotions and fragrances to consumers. The South Coast Plaza location, where I worked, was selected to be a test site for the brand extension, and I was selected to be part of that training. I learned and gained invaluable information that prepped me for and gave me even more insight into the world of retail.

Shortly after completing the training, I felt an even stronger desire to follow the fashion, which, for me, meant moving to New York City. NYC was the fashion capitol of the world and

1

FROM STILETTOS TO THE STOCK EXCHANGE

Childhood drawing

I wanted to immerse myself in the scene and culture. I knew since the fourth grade, when I drew a picture of myself in front of the New York City skyline with a briefcase and a town car that I would eventually move there. I followed that feeling – of learning more about fashion – and flew out to NY to interview for a position. With first-hand knowledge on the new line of fragrances and lotions, which hadn't debuted at the flagship Manhattan store, I was a bit of a commodity. I was hired, on the spot, to work as the store's assistant manager. I was ready to take what I knew and learned about branding and sales and apply it in a similar – although somewhat new – environment. What I wasn't ready for was the weather. I wasn't ready in the slightest.

I often tell people that I am a slave to the fashion and my initial experiences in New York prove it. On my first day at VS, I walked to work in heels. Now that may not sound strange to most, but if you've lived in New York, have worked in New York, or even visited the city, then you know maneuvering around in heels was a big risk to take, a 'no-no' in some circles. Oh, and did I mention that it was the middle of one of the worst winters in history when I started? A big 'no-no' indeed. But I couldn't help it and I didn't know any better. I refused to be the woman who traveled in a two-piece suit looking sharp from head to ankles, with a pair of sneakers adorning her feet. That just didn't make sense to me, no matter how smart or convenient it might have been. You can blame it on me being a recent Cali transplant, used to the sun and sand, and the freedom to wear what I wanted when I wanted to. You can also blame it on my image of fashion and staying true to that image at all costs. Any way you slice it, I had no idea what I was walking into and onto, literally. Within blocks of my destination, I fell while crossing the street, spilling everything in my purse onto the ground and slightly bruising my body and my pride. I had slipped on black ice and was shocked that no one stopped to help me. Maybe it was the heels? One thing is for sure: I learned a valuable lesson on knowing your environment and adapting.

Thankfully, that first day on my way to the job wasn't a reflection of what my time in New York would be like. If anything, it was the opposite. To be quite honest, no falls, trips, or bruises would stop me from taking hold of my dreams and succeeding. I had experienced far worse situations in the first quarter of my life and found the strength to pick myself up each time. I knew that I was not the sole beneficiary of my successes and failures and this drove me to push that much harder. I had a family in California rooting for and looking up to me. In our minds, my move to the "Big Apple" meant we had all made it. I was determined to make it for myself and for those whose blood coursed through my veins. Success wasn't an option; it was the only choice I had.

> If I can make it there, I can
> make it anywhere. It's up to
> you, New York New York.
> ~ excerpt from *New York, New York* by Frank Sinatra

Confidence Is KING

> "Whatever you can do or dream
> you can, begin it.
> Boldness has genius power
> and magic in it."
> – Johann von Goethe

My mother had always told me that I was smart, I was pretty, and that I could do what others did, but better. Thankfully, I listened and believed her. She had instilled confidence in me at an early age and that self-assurance helped me to navigate through my professional career and personal relationships. I didn't have a hard time adjusting to life in New York and gained ground at Victoria's Secret in a matter of months. I still hadn't learned my lesson with heels though and continued to peruse the streets in my pumps. The way I saw it, I was an extension of what I was selling. Equally important as the product was the person convincing the customer to make the purchase. I had to be polished and presentable every step of the way and my pumps were a part of the package. Besides, when you work for a company such as Victoria's Secret, where sexiness, sensuality, and celebrating the female body are the culture, living up to and embracing that culture becomes a necessity. To me, heels were, and still are, sexy and added even more edge and appeal to every woman. In short, they're part of my uniform.

Me and Mom in New Buffalo Michigan feeding geese

Me and Mom, 2010

FOLLOW THE FASHION, FOLLOW THE PASSION

Hey pretty baby with the high heels on
you give me fever like
I've never, ever known.
~ excerpt from *The Way You Make Me Feel* by Michael Jackson

I stayed on with Victoria's Secret for two years, long enough to be crowned "the Bra Queen." This was an in-house title that was given to the store's top sellers and I could sell some bras! From the reluctant to the risqué to the men looking to surprise their lady with no clue of a size, hardly anyone I worked with walked away empty handed. It was really about listening to the customer's needs and wants and finding a solution even when they didn't have the answers. And there were always answers; I just had to be creative to bring them out. When the men would come in, clueless and nervous without the slightest inkling of measurements, I'd grab a few lovely associates as models and ask the customer if any of the ladies were similar in size to his woman. I even used myself as an example. Without doubt, we would nail down the size and eventually, see the gentlemen go from embarrassed and nerve-wrecked to calm and assured. In many ways, I saw myself as a pseudo-counselor. I was there to ask the 'tough' questions and walk the customer through the process of 'discovering' and 'enjoying' lingerie shopping. Now that I think about it, a more accurate title would have been: Dr. Feel-Good Tina.

Things were going well in the Land of Lace, and I grew more confident in my position by the day. As one of the managers, I would often come in at 6 a.m. to open the store. One morning, shortly after walking in, I discovered that the upstairs stockroom was flooded. I panicked as there was an art gallery one level below us, the famous Pace Art Gallery, with clients such as Gianni Versace and I feared their art would be ruined. I called 911 and waited for help to come. Within 15 minutes, I heard sirens wailing through the Manhattan streets. I looked out the window and saw three fire trucks with firemen dressed in complete uniform. I went downstairs to let them in and explained to the chief what was going on. I felt bad as I didn't realize the whole fire department would be sent out to handle a flooded stockroom. When I asked the chief why they sent so many fire trucks out, he said that once they heard there was a situation at Victoria's Secret, none of the firefighters wanted to miss out. I didn't know my phone call would cause such a fuss, but the firefighters didn't seem to mind.

I loved working for Victoria's Secret and looked forward to special occasions, holidays, and events. This was especially the case during the busiest time of the year, which for our company, was Valentine's Day. We were a day or two away from the holiday when a news crew came to our location to get the juice on hot and popular items, trends for the season, and other recommendations for those still looking to get a gift or probably more accurate, to be the gift. The company spokesperson was not available, so I was asked to fill in for her. I had wrapped our segment when my phone started to vibrate. As I looked at the screen, I saw that it was my friend, Christina, calling. She wasted no time in sharing with me the nature of her call. "Tina, I am working for an up-and-coming designer, Max Azria, who launched a new company called

BCBG. I'm working for him. Tina, this company is going to explode," she said. I managed to squeeze in a, "That's great!"

"But that's not the great part," she continued. "He just opened up the same position that I hold here in L.A. in New York. They need someone great enough to do the job. I want you to set up an interview. When they offer you the job, I want you to say "yes." I want you to say "yes." I want you to say "ye-"" "Alright," I said before giving her the chance to finish saying that last "yes." She promised to send me the details and we both hung up the phone in excitement. I looked at my phone and smiled. I closed my eyes and felt the adrenaline, the rush of possibility and potential energy invade every cell of my body. I was floating and in that moment, felt like I was on top of the world. I wasn't looking to leave Victoria's Secret at that time, but if Christina was right about this new company "blowing up," I definitely wanted to be part of the explosion. I took a deep breath in and looked around as I let my breath escape through slightly opened lips. I just knew that I was going to make it. I was determined to do so anyway.

> "The question is not who
> is going to let me, it's
> who is going to stop me."
> – Ayn Rand

1980 - With Dad at a federal prison in Arizona visiting Richard

FOLLOW THE FASHION, FOLLOW THE PASSION

In the summer of 1980, Angela, Rocky, and I spent the summer months in Arizona with our father, as our parents were separated. As our time with our dad drew to an end, I couldn't bare the thought of leaving him and returning to my mother's house. I couldn't stomach being around her friends, the "Wastoids," as we called them. When the time came for us to return to California, I decided to stay behind with my dad. He was dating a 21-year-old woman at the time and she was pregnant with my father's child, a girl named Dyane. Admittedly, I wasn't the least bit happy about this as I now had one more person to compete with for my father's attention.

After Dyane was born, shortly before my 13th birthday, we moved from Arizona and went on a multi-state crime spree. My dad stole a printing machine and payroll checks, and within days we were creating counterfeit checks and cashing them. I learned how to use and mastered the printing machine, and would forge the checks with my dad. His girlfriend and I would cash them at grocery stores in each state. I had no idea why, at the time, I thought it was better to live with my father. His girlfriend and I always argued and I was terribly jealous of their new baby. Plus, we were all shoved in a van, committing crimes. All this to avoid my mom and her friends?

We landed in Oklahoma where we stayed with my dad's girlfriend's family. I hated being around them. The anger that had been simmering throughout my childhood because of my parents' separation and an incident on the beach that left third-degree burns on my feet was at a hard boil by this point. I felt rage like I never had before. I took the bus to an all-black school and felt completely out of place because I was the only Latina there. Weeks later when my dad discovered that it was an all-black school, he flipped out and said I was never going back. "You know enough," he said. I did not attend eighth grade. I was cool with not going to school and befriended a 20-year-old woman from the neighborhood. I hung out with her everyday, and together we'd hang out with guys. We continued on with our daily hangouts until my dad caught me. He beat the shit out of this one young man that I was kissing outside the library. Seriously, what did my dad expect? A 13-year-old girl not enrolled in school spells T-R-O-U-B-L-E in anyone's book.

Eventually, my grandfather, Jesus Cesar Aldatz, died. Since my father was a "wanted man," he could not attend the funeral. But he sent me back to California on his behalf. I was devastated. There were police and federal agents at my grandfather's funeral waiting for my father to show up. I never went back to live with him. Instead I rejoined my mom, my sister Angela, and my brother Rocky.

We were clueless as to where my father was and how he was doing. In 1986 (I was 18 years old) I found out that my dad was back in California and dating a different woman, someone six months younger than me. My dad, who was 45 at the time, was known for being a womanizer and did not have the best track record when it came to relationships. He would often become jealous and possessive, which would lead to physical abuse. I had witnessed this firsthand with my mother, Phylis, and in his relationship with Dyane's mother. My mother and my dad's

Dad with Holly

girlfriends were the recipients of multiple black eyes and bruises on their bodies because of my father's rage and insecurity. Each relationship was a tumultuous one that ended without him killing either woman as he so often threatened to do. My father was a career criminal, part-time drug dealer, part of a gang, and a talented carpenter and construction worker. He had a reputation for "being a bad ass" that preceded and followed him. For the life of me, I could not understand what my dad – who was back living in East Los Angeles under an alias name – saw in a 17-year-old white girl from the neighborhood. I equally couldn't comprehend what Holly, the young woman, would want with someone twice her age: someone who was old enough to be her father. I didn't know at the time that him being old enough to be her father was what attracted her to him.

I was so upset with the both of them for what I thought was a reckless and irresponsible decision. She had dated my cousin, which everyone – including my dad – knew about, before dating my father. I was so freaked out that this chick was my age. I just wanted my dad to myself. I stopped coming around as much and found it best to love my father from a distance.

FOLLOW THE FASHION, FOLLOW THE PASSION

*Papa was a rolling stone wherever he laid his hat was
his home and when he died all he left us was alone.*
~ excerpt from *Papa Was a Rolling Stone* by The Temptations

My anger subsided some once I received news that Holly, my dad's latest girlfriend, was pregnant with their first child. Little did I know that children would keep coming along consistently, starting with Richard in 1987, Kady in 1990, and Eric in 1992. On top of that, Angela gave birth to my niece in 1991 and Rocky had a son a few years later in 1995. These were the "Aldatz Family Baby Boomer Years." As much as I loved my family, I was still pissed. You could say that I was embarrassed and angry because of my dad's relationship with a woman young enough to be my sister, because no one was married, and because no one finished high school. I had started to see a cycle. I eventually realized that being upset with my father hurt me more than it hurt him. Instead, I wanted to be a part of my brothers' and sisters' lives. I wanted them to know that they were loved regardless of the situation and environment they were born into. Besides, neither my father nor his girlfriend was in the frame of mind or financial position to raise children properly.

Angela and I would visit and bring either toys or clothes for "the kids." We loved them dearly and had determined that we were going to give them as much of a better life as we could. We were going to stick together. Unfortunately, we lost contact with Dyane and her mother – my dad's girlfriend during the crime spree – who still lived in Oklahoma. A few decades later, after my dad died, Dyane and I reconnected. Dyane was raised in a loving and healthy environment, and grew to become a successful, beautiful, and smart woman. I apologized in person to Dyane's mother for all the grief I'm sure I caused her. She assured me that I had nothing to be sorry for because I was a child and didn't know any better. I was grateful to make amends and glad Dyane was raised by a strong woman.

By the time I turned 21 years old, my dad's girlfriend gave birth to my youngest sister, Kady. We all lived in Palm Springs, about three hours south of Whittier, with the exception of my mom, who was still in Orange County. I had opened a few vintage fashion stores in the area, my first go at entrepreneurship. My sister and I worked our butts off to support each other and her baby, my only niece, while sharing money with our father, who was in between jobs mostly. He started building gas stations in Palm Springs and brought out my uncle David and Rocky to help. Every so often he would luck up and get work on a construction site, but it never grew into substantial, long-term work. He was no longer gang-banging, but was still drinking and gambling, which is where most of his money went. Since I was nearby, I felt we had a pretty good life going for a while. The Denim X Change – my vintage stores – was doing well and our clientele grew to include celebrities. The stores were popular in that there wasn't any other store quite like it. In fact, we were around before there was a Buffalo Exchange. People would bring in their used Levi's and other denim brands. It was the early 90s and Hip-Hop was building more of a presence. Bold, bright colors were the style and spray paint was in. Think about the styles of early 1990s music groups such as T.L.C. I had an artist on hand who would do custom spray painting for any customer who wanted it on their shirts, jeans, hats, and the like. Denim X Change developed a huge and loyal following. We were well-known in the Palm Springs community and as far out as Los Angeles. We collaborated with local nightclubs to host fashion shows and other events.

At the age of 24, I had been living in Palm Springs for three years. I broke up with my boyfriend who funded the vintage clothing stores. I disapproved of his business practices and lost all respect for him when I discovered that he was a crook and a phony. He would attempt to control me with money and by buying me expensive gifts and he would treat people as if they were peasants because he had money and they didn't. I didn't like his true colors and broke off our relationship. He was heartbroken and as revenge, insisted I could not take a dime from the businesses with me. I had to leave everything – except for what I could fit in my 1974 red Volkswagen Karmann Ghia – behind, including my family. I drove to Costa Mesa and stayed with my friend JJ's older sister, Kristy and her husband. I had to start all over again with just the clothes on my back. Within a few months, everyone migrated back to Whittier and I had to help get them into an apartment. I started working at Victoria's Secret as a sales associate and signed the lease on an apartment for my dad, his girlfriend, and my three younger siblings which now included my youngest brother, Eric, who was born shortly before my family relocated to Whittier. Times were rough and it was extremely hard on me to continue supporting my family – let alone myself – in California with the amount of money I was making. I knew as long as I had the will, there would be a way. I was willing to do what I needed to do, within reason of course, to take care of my family. Angela and I moved into an apartment across from our mother so that we could share expenses. When I made the leap and moved to New York, it eased the financial burden of taking care of my family simply because of the change in the cost of living. I made more money, which meant I could send more money home. When things became better for me, things subsequently became better for my family, which was my desire.

> Some dreams are in the nighttime and some seem like yesterday.
> But leaves turn brown and fade. Ships sail away.
> You long to say a thousand words, but seasons change.
> ~ excerpt from *Seasons Change* by Expose

We were sitting in bumper-to-bumper traffic with horns blaring and honking from every direction. My boyfriend of one year, Joey, was taking me to my second interview with the BCBG Company. I met Joey through my Dominican friend China while out with her and her model boyfriend at a nightclub in New York. Her boyfriend's best friend, Joey, was DJ'ing that night. We were introduced and immediately hit it off. Since Joey was a DJ, we were able to get into all of the hottest parties and clubs every night. I was living the New York life, working for the hottest lingerie store in the world, and dating one of the biggest names in Hip-Hop, which was pretty funny since Hip-Hop really wasn't my scene. The girls at Victoria's Secret were shocked when Joey came to pick me up from work one day, wearing baggy clothes with a diamond on his tooth. No one ever expected me to date someone who looked, dressed, and was in the music industry like Joey.

I had called out sick from Victoria's Secret so that I could go on my BCBG interview during lunchtime. I made it through the initial interview with ease and was about to meet with Max Azria and his brother at the New York office. Before anyone was hired to work for the company, Max Azria had to meet and interview with the potential hire first. Max flew in from Los Angeles to meet with me, which was a pretty big deal, and I was nervous. I was rehearsing my answers in my mind, thinking of any and all of the questions he could ask me. All of a sudden Joey's voice jolted me back to the present moment. "Hey man, what are you doing?!" he yelled out to the cab driver in front of us. The driver had cut us off and Joey was fuming. "Just leave it alone Joey," I said. "It really is OK." Joey didn't listen and continued to exchange words with the driver. Within seconds, both men got out of their cars and their words grew even more heated. As I got out of the car to try to talk some sense back into Joey, a fistfight ensued between the two. Though the timing wasn't great, I was secretly proud of him for winning the fight. I thought it was 'hot' because it showed that he was a tough guy. Maybe in that moment he reminded me a bit of my father.

"Damn it, I really don't need this today," I thought as I screamed and yelled at Joey to stop. The police came and broke up the fight and took both men to jail. I followed behind the squad cars trying my best to maintain my peace of mind and sanity amongst the madness. Of all the days to get in a fight, Joey had to pick today. He knew how important this interview was and the opportunities it would afford and open up for us. In his mind, his actions were justified as he was protecting me. But in my mind, he was adding unwanted and unnecessary drama to my life. Thankfully, he was released shortly after I posted bail and the whole ordeal only set me back by an hour or two. I managed to shake off the drama of the morning and refocus on the task at hand. I arrived to the BCBG office in Manhattan a few minutes ahead of my interview. I felt that all-too-familiar feeling of nervousness and anxiety creep up. For once, I welcomed it with open arms. After all, it beat being upset or angry at Joey.

I waited in the lobby – with its plush leather seating and ambiance – for less than 10 minutes when the receptionist escorted me to the back. Goosebumps percolated along my body. I knew this was the break I needed. I had a gut feeling that my life was about to change. The walk from the lobby to the interview room was hardly even 20 feet but to me, it felt like a mile. I went inside and took a seat at the desk. I could hardly contain the intensity in my heart and felt that Max and his brother could even hear it beating wildly against my chest. Neither Max nor his brother said anything outside of "hello." They looked through my file and for a moment, seemed oblivious to me being there.

After a few minutes, Max broke the silence. He looked up at me and asked in a thick, French-Tunisian accent, "What is your sign?" I sat there dumbfounded. "Did he really ask me what I think he did?" I thought. "Excuse me?" I asked out loud. He repeated the question. "Um, I am a Sagittarius," I responded, still in shock at the question. I was expecting him to ask me about my work history, what I knew about the company, my work ethic – not what my astrological sign was. "Hmm…OK," he responded. "OK?" I asked. I was confused. "OK, I like you. You are hired," he said. He, along with his brother, stood up and welcomed me to the company. I stood there a bit dazed. I could not believe what had just happened. I managed to say "thank you" and talked a little about the details of the position. I was happy to be on board and still a bit surprised at how easy it was. As I walked down the hall towards the lobby, the receptionist said, "He's a bit eccentric, isn't he?" She must have read my facial expression. "Yes he is," I said with a smile. As I walked onto the elevator, happy with the direction my life was going, I remembered that I had to give my notice to Victoria's Secret, my security blanket. Gulp.

ONWARD AND UPWARD

I delved into the world of BCBG head first, ready to win, and dressed to impress. I was the new Merchandising Director for the East Coast and traveled extensively from NYC to Chicago to Miami. As the merchandising director, I was responsible for building in-store shops and displays with clients such as Bloomingdales and product assortment, I had to choose the right assortment of clothing for every location. For example, the clothes that might sell in February in Los Angeles or Miami would not sell in Chicago or New York City because of the difference in weather. I loved my job and learned more about the fashion industry than I initially imagined. Since I worked in fashion, I had the freedom to dress fashionably. I dressed in the BCBG collection – from head to toe – everyday and wore pumps all the time since I had a clothing allowance with BCBG, which was included in my salary. I looked amazing. My feet, however, felt anything but amazing. With the increase in walking around New York, traveling from city to city, and installing new displays – all in heels – my feet were taking a serious beating. I would frequent the shoe repair shops once a week for insoles to lessen the pain I was feeling. Although the insoles provided temporary relief, they were ugly and bulky. I didn't think comfort had to come at the expense of appeal, but every product on the market seemed to say just that: comfort without style. I sucked it up and continued to buy the insoles because I didn't have another choice. If I wanted to do my job effectively and thoroughly, I had to make sure my feet were happy with me. I just wished there was a way for my feet to be happy AND sexy too.

My role at BCBG morphed with time, as Max would allow me to be creative with special projects that stretched me beyond my job description. I was tapped to coordinate and execute BCBG in-store shops and promotional events, and I helped with fashion shows in New York and globally. I was sent to London – along with my new best friend and coworker Margie Floris – to orchestrate the company's first international press and marketing event. I met Margie my first few days at BCBG. She was not happy with most of the changes I was implementing in the department and confronted me about it. We had gotten into such a heated debate that our boss had to step in and quell the argument before it became something more. A week later, on payday, I asked if anyone knew how to send money out of state as I needed to wire money to my family. Margie, who hadn't really spoken to me since our confrontation said, "Come with me." She was on her way to Western Union to send money to her family in Spain. She had a "VIP" card, so we didn't have to wait in line. She showed and walked me through the process of wiring money. We became friends at that moment. Margie and I were the only Latinas who worked in the New York showroom. This shared experience deepened our friendship. We were entrenched in the business of BCBG and only grew closer while in London. We became like sisters and realized we had more similar interests and responsibilities than we initially expected.

> I'll reach out my hand to you
> I'll have faith in all you do
> Just call my name and I'll be there
> ~ excerpt from *I'll Be There* by the Jackson 5

The company continued to grow and establish a solid reputation for itself as a fashion house that was not going out of style. I was completely invested in BCBG and did my job because it was easy and lots of fun. There were challenges and hard work but I enjoyed every bit of it. It helped that I was surrounded by an amazing team of supportive and great leaders. Their greatness sharpened me and inspired me to be great. I was happy with my life and for once, felt things were on the up in all areas.

One day, Joey and I were out going for our routine walk with our dog, Casper, a white pit bull. Joey seemed a bit hesitant and was out of character, but I didn't think too much about it. "We need to break up," Joey said out of the blue, causing me to stop mid-stride.

"What, why?" I asked. I didn't understand where it was coming from as everything was going well in our three-year relationship. I thought we were going to get married. My relationship with Joey was the first time I had loved anyone enough to imagine being married.

"I…we just need to break up," he said. I wasn't convinced.

"What the fuck are you saying?" I responded, trying to figure out what led to this. No one had ever broken up with me before. I was so shocked and out of it that I could have been knocked over with a feather! In that moment I knew what had happened. We couldn't be together because I was not Armenian. Joey was raised in a traditional Armenian family and he was expected to marry a woman within his culture. I was infuriated but more than anything, I was hurt. I quickly

13

put the upscale, New York Tina to the side and brought out the Art's daughter from East Los Angeles Tina. When Joey informed me that he intended to stay at the apartment until he found a new place to live, I started to plot my revenge.

"Fine," I said. "But let me warn you that I cannot be responsible for anything that happens to you or your shit." Joey had over $10,000 worth of musical equipment and priceless records. The next morning, while he lay asleep on the couch, I filled a huge pitcher of ice water and poured it all over him. I ran out of the apartment and caught the train to work. Sweet satisfaction. There was no point in waiting around for someone who knew we couldn't go further than girlfriend and boyfriend. No, there was no turning back. There was too much good waiting ahead for me. Fuck it.

I moved to the Murray Hill neighborhood on 33rd and 3rd, which was only two blocks away from Margie. I was still saddened by my breakup but had the comfort of my best friend being so close to me, and a job that kept me busy and focused. I eventually met and fell in love with a married man, which was a disaster from the start. I was emotionally involved and had become so close to him in a short amount of time. He was the love of my life, but I knew our relationship couldn't and wouldn't go anywhere. When Paula Schneider, president of Sales, approached me with an offer to move back to California to head up special events alongside Max Azria's wife Lubov, I accepted as it was a new challenge and would bring me closer to my family. And with the emotional ties I had to this married man, I needed a way out. After five years in New York City, it was time to go home.

Please darlin' don't you cry.
Let's just kiss and say goodbye.
~ excerpt from *Kiss and Say Goodbye* by The Manhattans

Me and Rocky, 2007

CHAPTER TWO

A Beautiful Mess

I walked out of LAX airport and saw palm trees, clear blue skies, and lots of sunshine. As much as I loved New York, it could not compare to the consistently pleasant weather and the beautiful scenery in California. I was back on my native soil, taking in the sights, the sounds, and the smells. It had been about a year since my last visit and I was curious to see what, if anything, had changed. From what I could tell, everything remained the same; but then again, I was still at the airport.

A black 4-door Lexus pulled up to the curb. The passenger door window lowered and revealed a waving hand. I peaked inside and saw two rather dashing young men looking at me. I smiled as my younger brother Rocky stepped out of the car and gave me a kiss. "Look at you," we both said to each other. "Nice wheels," I said before he informed me that it was his friend Jason's new ride. Whenever I came home, Rocky and his friends would come scoop me up from the airport, no matter the length of my stay or where I needed to go. It was our ritual and I looked forward to hanging with the guys any time I came home for a visit. I didn't start work for another week so I had a couple days to hang out with my family before temporarily moving in with my friend and new boss, Paula. She was gracious enough to let me stay at her house until my apartment was ready. As much as I wanted to be closer to my family, the 120-minute, one-way daily commute from Laguna Beach where they lived to Los Angeles would have been a bit of a stretch, especially with my work schedule.

The drive down to Laguna Beach provided Rocky, Jason and me enough time to catch each other up on life, family, and work. Rocky was working as a stockbroker and was a relatively new dad. I couldn't wait to get my hands on my 2-year-old nephew; I love babies! I was a bit hesitant to see my mom as I hadn't talked with her in about six months. She had come out to New York with her best friend Roberta to attend Roberta's son's graduation from West Point. They both stayed at my studio apartment. At first, it was all fun and games and laughter. Then, in typical Phylis fashion, she began to get on my nerves repeatedly. Roberta paid for my mother's trip to New York so that she could attend the graduation with her. They rented a car, got stoned, and decided my mom would navigate their drive from New York City to West Point. They were so out of it that they missed the main ceremony. Roberta was livid. Once they returned to the city, I took them out to a few nightspots and bars. In hindsight, it was a disaster waiting to happen. Each place we went to, my mom caused a scene. She started with the whistling. Now, this wasn't just a normal whistle. It was a piercing two-fingers-under-the-tongue-and-a-hard-blow-ugly-face-fucking whistle that, to this day, makes me cringe. I had heard that whistle my entire life. My mom would whistle to get us to come home when my siblings and I were younger, out playing in the neighborhood. I resented that whistle as it made me feel like a dog. Phylis was known as the "Queen of Whistles" when she was younger so imagine how much she had mastered it by her adult years. She kept whistling and was obnoxious and loud the entire time. She didn't know how to chill and enjoy the evening without being a spectacle herself. Then, to top it off, after seeing a play on Broadway, she spots actor Elliott Gould, goes up to him in a creepy, stalker-like manner, grabs him by the arm, and screams, "Is that really you?" I nearly died. If embarrassment was a cause of death, it would have definitely been the cause that night. She sensed that I was irritated and went on to call me "Ms. Hollywood" and "Ms. Drama Queen" simply because I wouldn't engage in her shenanigans. We got into a huge argument where I called her "white trash" as my mom is half Danish, half Irish and she flipped it back on me and asked, "So what does that make you?" I was so heated and hurt by her words that I left them at the bar. I went and stayed at my neighbor Marci's place, which was a few floors down from my apartment. I stayed over Marci's for one night and returned to my apartment the following morning. I was partially relieved once I realized my mom and her friend weren't there. My mother left New York without saying "goodbye" and I hadn't talked with her since. As much as I loved her, our relationship had its moments of strain and grief. She was one of a few people who knew how to get under my skin and hurt me.

Clowns to the left of me Jokers to the right
Here I am stuck in the middle with you.
~ excerpt from *Stuck In the Middle With You* by by Stealers Wheel

Between my dad's chosen gang and drug lifestyle and my mom's alcoholism and excessive partying, I had witnessed more than my fair share of drama in my childhood and adolescent years. I only hoped that the drama would lessen as I – rather we – got older. What I found was that the expression, "Old habits die hard," is very true. I sincerely wanted a better life for my parents, siblings, and relatives than the one we experienced growing up. I had to learn and accept that my desire for a better life for my family was futile and meant nothing if they didn't want it for themselves. This was a very hard lesson for me to embrace.

The year was 1966, two years before I was born. There was a party at one of the local bars in Pico Riviera, California, and since he was just released from jail, my father Art decided to check it out. He walked in – 5'9", soft spoken, and with a powerful presence. My mother, who was the only blond there, stood against the wall talking with one of her girlfriends. She looked up and saw my father and became enamored with his handsome features. My father returned the stare, in awe of this beautiful, statured woman before him. They locked eyes and soon after, my dad walked towards her to strike up a conversation. A week later, my father – along with his brother, David – went over to my mom and her best friend's, Susie, apartment. My dad wanted his brother to meet Susie so that they could all hang out. As our mother would later tell us, it was "history" after that. The brothers fell in love with the best friends. Within months, my dad married my mother, and my Uncle David married Susie. My mom and Susie were living a dream as they both wanted to marry brothers and raise their kids together.

Angela, Dad and me
in front of our home
in New Buffalo

My parents moved to New Buffalo, Michigan, within a month of their wedding and bought a house. They had relocated to New Buffalo for my dad's new job at Woodrow & Sons Construction Company. The move provided my parents a fresh start away from the East Los Angeles gangs, violence, and temptation of drugs and alcohol. My mom was a hairstylist from California which made her a bit of a celebrity. The women lined up at the salon just so that my mom could style their hair like "the women in California." With my mom's vibrant personality, beautiful features, and penchant for making clients feel good in their own skin, she had developed a loyal base of regular customers. My dad was also the center of much talk and admiration. He was a bit of a rarity in New Buffalo as he was Mexican and most of the townspeople had never seen a Mexican before. On top of that, he walked around shirtless with chest and bulging muscles exposing his tattoos. Together, my parents were considered "the beautiful people," a title that went beyond mere physical features to describing what they did for others: they made things and people beautiful. Once Angela and I were born, 1970 and 1968 respectively, our family became known as the beautiful clan. As we got a little older, my mom would bring us into the salon every week where she would primp and curl our hair and polish our nails red. She didn't mind us wearing our hair the way we wanted. She never flinched at us asking for red polish. She wanted us to embrace what made us happy and to ask for what we wanted. We were polished and pretty little girls who always had to have our hair and nails "just right." Even to this day, I go crazy if my ponytail is not smooth at the roots and has a "bump" on it. I no longer lay on the floor, kicking and screaming until the bump is fixed though.

We traveled quite a bit in our formative years as my dad's work would lead him to new cities. When I was around four years old, we moved to Tucson, Arizona, where my dad started building houses. He came aboard at the start of the "tract house trend" where they built similar looking houses on a plot of land. Angela and I would go to the site with our mom and watch our father build what eventually would become our house. Although most of the houses looked alike, we found a way to make ours stand out. Our father placed a huge boulder on our front lawn that complemented the well-landscaped yard. There was no way of mistaking "The Aldatz House" as my dad took pride in ownership, a trait that has stuck with me. Everything he did was meticulous.

There was a difference in Tucson living than what we experienced in New Buffalo that didn't take long to notice. In New Buffalo, our family was well-liked and genuinely well-received; in Tucson, there was a lot of jealousy and envy directed toward us, especially at my mom. My dad was handsome and handy which made him even more appealing and enticing to the women in the neighborhood. Around the time my brother was born, my parents started to get into frequent arguments over what my mom said was my dad's "womanizing ways." The women were relentless and would throw themselves at my father. It didn't help that he would walk around shirtless, which only fueled their desire for him even more. Every other day some woman would need a "favor" and would sashay around my dad. I didn't like it one bit and could tell, even at age six that something wasn't right about it. I also knew that the way those women acted towards my father and how he responded to them led to long, drawn-out fights between my parents. Despite his love for his family, my father couldn't seem to resist the temptation of flirting and messing around with other women. Even my friend, who was six just like me, shared that she, too, had a crush on my dad! Whenever my dad drove me to school, he'd pick up my friends along the way and she was one of them. After she shared her secret with me, I became so upset that I cut her out of the carpool. I couldn't stand it when anyone else vied for my dad's attention and found it disrespectful.

> Now I know all the girls I've seen you with
> I know you broke their hearts one after another now
> Bit by bit, you made em cry
> When they tried to keep you happy
> they just tried to keep you satisfied
> Mr. Bigstuff – who do you think you are?
> ~ excerpt from *Mr. Bigstuff* by Jean Knight

A year or two into living in Tucson, my older cousin Richard was sent to live with our family. Richard was my dad's nephew, and he was sent to my father so that he could distance himself from the East Los Angeles gangs and get "straightened out." My dad was happy to have Richard with him, and helped him to learn the ins and outs of construction. Richard was able to secure a job with my father, and at 17 years old, was showing some improvements. A day before his 18th birthday, Richard committed a crime and was sentenced to repeated life sentences in maximum-security prison. Our entire family was devastated and for the longest time, my dad blamed himself for Richard's actions. Richard was supposed to turn his life around, and in my dad's eyes, he was to see to it that Richard changed. Living in Tucson was supposed to be Richard's second chance, a fresh start from the East Los Angeles gang culture. Richard was young, handsome, athletic, and poised to be the next Golden Gloves contender and a ruler in the streets of L.A. He had a big chip on his shoulder and felt invincible. In a fit of rebellion, Richard stole my dad's truck while we were sleeping. He went out to have some fun, which led to a bar and a woman who was looking for a good time, which led to a hotel room, a pimp, and a gun. The events of that night turned our world upside down. My parents and extended family spent everything they had on lawyers in hopes of getting Richard out of prison to no avail. We ended up spending the next 25 years visiting my beloved cousin in prison.

At the age of seven, one year after Rocky was born, we moved to Chino, California, where my dad accepted a position as a construction foreman. We had another cool house that I absolutely adored. The house was a Spanish hacienda-inspired, white, ranch-style structure with wrought iron. The move gave my parents a fresh start, and my admiration for my father only grew deeper. My dad would rise at 5 a.m. and sit in the kitchen to fill out his reports. I would join, cross-legged, at the dining room table, helping him spell out the words he didn't know. We both drank our coffee with milk and sugar, and I would mimic his every move. This became our morning ritual, our special time together. I cherished that time with my entire being. My dad only had a ninth grade education, if that, and was gifted in math. He was a craftsman and artist at heart who believed that "Mexicans can actually fix anything out of just a roll of duct tape." I found it silly every time he said that, but figured he may have been on to something.

We pulled up to Angela's apartment in Laguna, which is where I stayed my first weekend back in Cali. She already had a full house with her daughter, boyfriend, and our mother living there, which was another reason I opted to stay with Paula until my rent-controlled apartment was ready. I was happy to be home with my family and thankfully everyone was in a good mood. I got to spend quality time with my brothers and sisters, niece and nephew, and relax and chill out for a few days, which I needed. I ate well, too. There's nothing like breaking bread with family. There is something about home-cooked meals that trumps eating out at restaurants any day. Every day was a feast: tortillas, refried beans, carne de asada, rice, limes, beers, and so much more. The weekend helped me get grounded in Cali before diving into my new position at BCBG. I knew Max and Lubov were counting on me to help coordinate the company's marketing initiatives and lead the teams in globally delivering the brand message to the consumer, similar to what I did in New York. I was ready, pumped and motivated to get great results and to keep Max and Lubov happy. Besides, it's easy to do your best and be your best when you work for the best.

Sunday came without so much as a hiccup between my mother and I, which made it hard for me to leave. When things were bad, it was horrible; when things were good, it was great. The weekend was one of those great moments and I didn't want it to end. I reminded myself that I moved back to California for work; being closer to my family was an added incentive. My brother drove me up to Paula's house later that evening and I was a bit surprised at what I saw when we arrived. Paula's house was a mansion in the mountains of South Pasadena; a mansion! I had no idea. I kept looking at the paper with her address on it and it matched the numbers in front of the gate. I looked over at Rocky whose face mirrored my own. "Looks like I'm here," I said while leaning over to give him a kiss. I got out of the car and watched as he drove off.

I was not used to the lifestyle Paula lived but it didn't take me long to adjust. After Paula gave me a tour of her home, she showed me to my room – a fully furnished space of luxurious comfort. Paula had two daughters, Zoe and Chloe, who were very curious as to who I was and my reason for being in their home. Once they got used to me being there, they followed me around all the time. They reminded me of my younger siblings and niece. They quickly became my family away from family. If having my bedroom with a king-sized bed wasn't enough, I had access to Paula's maids too. They were very sweet and treated me like I was part of the family. I enjoyed everything I was experiencing and receiving at Paula's but I felt guilty when I started to think about my family. My new living environment was quite a contradiction to that of my family's.

Cause there's a place in the sun where there's hope for everyone. Where my poor restless heart's gotta run. There's a place in the sun. And before my life is done got to find me a place in the sun.

~ excerpt from *A Place in the Sun* by Stevie Wonder

THE BALANCING ACT

I walked into the L.A. offices to start my new job with BCBG as the Director of Promotional Marketing and Special Events. I was excited to get started. I had a fabulous office with an amazing, strong, diverse, and talented team. We were responsible for the overall growth of the company, specifically in cultivating B2B relationships. As a business-to-business (B2B) retailer, BCBG clothing was placed into major department stores such as Nordstrom's - I knew I'd find a way to work with them - Macy's, and the like; the revenue generated from those relationships fed the company the capital it needed to grow and eventually open more independent retail stores. I had arrived back in California in March, shortly after the spring runway shows in New York. My first order of business in Los Angeles was to coordinate a runway show on Rodeo Drive similar to the one in New York. We already had a sponsor secured – Mercedes Benz – so it was a matter of working out the logistics needed to execute the show. That was the fun part. From securing models to creating the show timeline to drafting the guest list, to curating gifts for VIPs, we had our work cut out for us. And we got it done. In less than a month, the show went up without a glitch. Max and Lubov were pleased and our guests kept talking about how well executed the show was. I was in my zone, doing what I loved, and soaking up all the praise and commendations for our hard work. Life was good and I felt as if I was on top of the world.

I wanted my younger siblings to be exposed to something new, a different environment than the one they were growing up in. On the weekends, Paula would take my car and I'd borrow her SUV. I would drive down to Whittier to pick up Richard, Kady, and Eric from my dad's place. I'd bring them back to Pasadena where they'd stay with me for the weekend, and play with Paula's two daughters. I was comfortable in Paula's home and it felt good to share a bit of my world with my siblings. They enjoyed the time and had fun with Zoe and Chloe. Seeing their faces light up with joy, their innocent smiles, and laughter enhanced my life; I felt happier having them there with me.

After two months, my apartment was finally ready but I wasn't. I had enjoyed living at Paula's and it felt good to be part of what I considered to be a normal functioning family. I was in no hurry to move and would have stayed there forever. When Paula insisted that I go ahead and move into my apartment, I realized that I had overstayed my welcome and that it was time to leave. I probably would have stayed longer if she hadn't said anything. I moved out of a mansion

Me, Richard, Kady
and Eric the week
before I moved to NYC

in South Pasadena where everything was provided for to a two-bedroom apartment in Santa Monica, where there was no one there to make me bagged breakfasts with my name on it; Paula's maids were the best! I spruced up my apartment and made it as much of a home as possible.

Shortly after moving into my apartment, my father started having issues again with his girlfriend, Holly – the mother of my three younger siblings Richard, Kady, and Eric. Things were going well it seemed. The kids were taken care of and in school, and my dad was able to keep a roof over their heads. Over time, Holly's family – who did not like my dad because he was much older and Mexican – stepped in. Holly's brothers jumped my father and kicked him out of his apartment. My dad was in love with Holly and refused to leave her, yet she had grown tired of him and his possessiveness. She was weak and helpless, which is why her family finally stepped in for her. I drove down to Whittier with my Uncle David to get my dad before someone ended up dead or in jail, again. I brought him back to Santa Monica with me but I knew his heart was in Whittier. I had heard him say many times before that she was the love of his life.

Over time, Holly started dating again and ended up in a new relationship to a man she would eventually have three children with. Her new boyfriend was not fond of my three younger siblings, which left them feeling unwanted in their own home. This new guy was a loud, fat, Mexican, crack head that would beat on their mother. He was known for abandoning her on the side of the road, barefoot and pregnant. He was a real class act. My siblings would often go hungry for days on end. I would drive down on the weekends to bring them back to Santa Monica where they could spend time with my father and me whenever he was around. They would open up to me on what was going on at home. Their mother's new boyfriend was physically abusive to her as well.

This is insane,
all you did was say hello...
whisper my name
How can it be we're in a different space and time
In a place I used to know long ago – déjà vu
Could you be the dream I once knew?
~ excerpt from *déjà vu* by Dionne Warwick

A few months into living in Santa Monica, I received a call from child services. My worst nightmare was unfolding before me. My siblings and their mom were at The Good Shepherd battered women's shelter in Los Angeles – the same fucking shelter my mom fled to with me, Angela, and Rocky in 1979. I was heartbroken, devastated, and deeply ashamed. There they were experiencing and living out the same childhood trauma that their older siblings did just under 20 years ago. I knew I had to do something. The courts threatened to place Richard, Kady, and Eric in foster care as their mom wasn't in the best mental, financial, and emotional condition to take care of them. I would not allow them to be placed in the system. I started to research the custody process, knowing that I could provide a more stable and loving home for my siblings. They did not have to continue to be subjected to the consequences of their mother's choices and reckless decisions. I registered with Live Scan – electronic fingerprinting for criminal record check – and started the long and uphill battle to obtain custody of my siblings.

My professional and personal lives started to overlap and thankfully I was able to balance it. Child services had become a regular visitor and brought my siblings to me at least twice a month. They couldn't be left alone so I'd take them in with me to the BCBG offices. Max and Lubov were well aware of my family situation and allowed me to bring them to work with me anytime I needed to. I'd have my siblings up to a week at a time before they were taken back to their mother. Within a week or two, something would happen and child services would bring them back to me. This cycle continued for months and I was becoming irritated with the custody process. I wanted my siblings to be with me but their mother did not. If I became the legal guardian of my siblings, then she would no longer receive welfare benefits. That was enough reason for her to fight any of my attempts to take custody, but it was not enough to help her turn her life around for the benefit of her kids. I was growing tired of my siblings going back and forth from their mother's apartment to my place; I wanted nothing more than a stable and secure life for them.

FROM STILETTOS TO THE STOCK EXCHANGE

I'm gonna make a change
for once in my life
It's gonna feel real good
gonna make a difference
Gonna make it right.
~ excerpt from *Man In the Mirror* by Michael Jackson

It was late afternoon in the summer of 1979 in Chino, California, and Rocky, Angela, and I were in our room getting ready for bed. Our parents were in the living room screaming and cussing at each other. We had just finished hosting a yard sale a couple hours earlier, which is where most of the arguing started. My mom had on short shorts and was a bit friendly towards some of the people who stopped by. There was a black guy who came with some friends and my mom kept talking with them. My dad, who was extremely racist, became incensed. He was pissed that my mom was even entertaining this guy and that she had on such short shorts. He started to drink alcohol; by the time the yard sale ended, my dad was drunk. We helped clean up and moved the remaining items from the yard sale inside our house. My dad instructed us to get ready for bed. The sun was starting to set and it was still pretty early, but we didn't argue back.

As we brushed our teeth, the yelling began in the living room. I heard a loud thud, in fact, multiple thuds and what sounded like something being slammed against the wall. By this point, my siblings and I were in bed but we couldn't sleep. We were used to the fights that would erupt between our parents but that night sounded different. My mom was Danish-Irish and my father was Mexican and Basque. They both had two different perspectives on how women should behave in relationships. My mom was very vocal, strong-minded, strong-willed, boisterous, and had a sharp tongue, witty. She came from a line of women who were used to running the household. My father was a traditional Mexican man and believed that a woman's place was at home, bearing and taking care of the children, cooking dinner, and being subservient to their husbands. My parents both had Type A personalities, which was an underlying contributing factor to their disagreements and fights. The screaming continued and I eventually got out of bed and went into the living room. Shards of glass lie haphazardly on the carpeted floor while the couch pillows were strewn across the tables. My mom's face was peppered with bruises, the blood streaming from her nose, her lip swollen from an apparent blow to her face. And there he stood, my father, with a gun pointed between my mom's eyes. He was beyond raged; one wrong move and one wrong word had the potential to shatter and tear apart our family forever. My mom kept screaming out "I hate you" at my dad. He stood there frozen, ready to pull the trigger at any moment. I walked to my father and stood in front of him. I held out my hand and said, "Daddy, give me the gun." He looked at me as my mom kept screaming, "I hate you" in the background. His eyes stayed locked in to mine. "Daddy, it's Tina…give me the gun," I repeated. I watched the look in his eyes go from incensed to sorrowful in a matter of minutes. "Oh mija,"

Mom and Grandma Betty

he said, handing the gun to me and falling to his knees. He wept while repeatedly saying, "Oh mija" between sobs. I was the only one who could get through to him during his rage. I hugged him and felt the disgust in my mother's voice as she continued to yell, "I hate you!"

Within seconds, my mom approached my dad with his sawed-off bat, the handle tightly wrapped with black electrical tape, and started to attack him. My dad got up and grabbed her; he took the bat from her and started to beat her with it. My mom blanked out and fell to the ground. My dad had hit her in the head; she had a gash on the left side of her head that started at her temple and reached halfway across her head into her scalp. Angela and I jumped on our father and tried to keep him off our mother. Rocky, who was only three years old at the time, ran to my mom and started to drag her out of the house to our neighbor's. The neighbor helped my mother inside their home and called the police and an ambulance. Fifteen minutes later, the police arrived and took my father to jail. My mom, who was in and out of consciousness, was placed on the gurney and wheeled into the ambulance. She was taken to the hospital. Child services picked up Rocky, Angela and me and took us to our maternal grandmother's, Grandma Betty, apartment.

I didn't know that day would be the last time our family lived together as a family, and it would be the last time we lived in a normal house. My mom stayed in the hospital for a week then came to stay with us at Grandma Betty's. A few weeks later, my father was released from jail. He started to drive by the apartment complex, yelling for my mom and us kids to come out. He was loud and determined to have us come outside, but we remained inside. He made frequent trips, sometimes multiple times in a day, to no avail. After one particular visit from my father where he waved a gun in the air while yelling for us to come out, my mom waited until he pulled off then went to the room where we were sleeping and started packing our clothes. She moved with haste and prompted us to do the same; we had no idea if and when my father would return. We left the apartment and fled to The Good Shepherd, a women's shelter in downtown Los Angeles. They took us in and we remained there with our mother for two years.

It's a thin line, between love and hate.
~ excerpt from *Thin Line Between Love and Hate* by The Persuaders

Since my father had threatened, and attempted, to kill our mother, we were under surveillance and could not leave the property. I was 10, Angela was eight, and Rocky was four when we first arrived; we adjusted to the shelter and made friends with some of the other kids who lived there. Our mother enrolled in *Chrysalis*, one of the shelter's programs, and learned how to assemble computer parts. After she completed the training, she secured a job in Control Data at the shelter.

We made the most out of the situation as best we could. While mom was at work, Angela, Rocky and I would run around and play our games. In our minds, the shelter was like a fortress; every day was a new adventure where we'd explore what was initially undiscovered territory. One time, Angela and I went to the basement and saw tables piled high with clothes, shoes, and accessories. Our eyes widened as we ran over to the table and excitedly started trying on any and everything we could get our hands on. There were so many bright-colored tops and dresses and big-brimmed hats. We were in heaven. Once fully dressed, we started walking down an imaginary runway. We just knew we were hot and no one could tell us otherwise. Our fashion show was interrupted when one of the shelter workers came downstairs carrying four large garbage bags. She opened the bags and dumped its contents on the tables. My mouth dropped and I became upset once I saw the clothes falling out of the bag onto the tables, and eventually onto the floor. We were wearing, playing, and modeling in someone else's garbage, someone else's hand-me-downs. I was embarrassed and immediately started to undress myself and instructed Angela to do the same. "We are not some charity case," I said to Angela as we ran upstairs to the living areas. I made a vow to myself and my sister that day that we were not going to be the recipient of someone else's trash. Even at 10 years old, my sense of Latino pride was strong. We never set foot in that basement again. There is a difference between accepting charity and using resources. This is a lesson I would figure out later in my life.

After a long and drawn out court process, the judge ruled in favor of me becoming 'Next of Kin' for my three younger siblings. The judge's decision was influenced by a character letter that Max Azria and several executives wrote on my behalf. In the letter, they shared in detail my upbringing and how I was determined to be successful and a positive role model in my siblings' lives. The judge agreed with Max's sentiments that my siblings deserved the chance to be in a healthy environment, one that supported their growth to being successful and productive citizens. As 'next of kin,' I was the legal guardian of my siblings whenever child services would take them from their mother. I was granted supervision of them whenever their mother was using drugs and in turbulent relationships that threatened my siblings' safety. I was grateful to be the official 'Next of Kin' and ready to be the best for them by any means necessary.

Me, Kady and Eric going to work at BCBG

Everyone can see
we're together
As we walk on by (FLY!)
and we fly just like
birds of a feather
I won't tell no lie.
~ excerpt from *We Are Family*,
by Sister Sledge

Me and Margie at BCBG Christmas Party 1998

CHAPTER THREE

$6,000 And a Dream

It was 1999 and I had been with BCBG for nearly six years. I had watched the company grow from a somewhat known designer to a global fashion house that everyone was talking about. As the company grew and became corporate, the infrastructure became more formal. Instead of having direct access to Max, Lubov, and Paula, I had to report to a new "head of this" or "head of that." I knew this was to the benefit of the company, but I did not like it. The fun, loving, and free environment I had become accustomed to was getting more formal by the day. I didn't see any advances I could take in the company; the only promotions would be linear, or to a position on the same level as mine. I had officially hit a glass ceiling within the company.

Leaving BCBG was one of the toughest decisions I had to make, but I knew I had to. BCBG was more than a place of business where I'd report for work, clock in, clock out, and go about my day. No. BCBG was a family, a community of creative and like-minded individuals all working toward a greater vision of fashion and expression. On a more personal level, the BCBG family stepped in and supported me any and every time I needed them, especially when my siblings were involved. I learned how to be a leader, was allowed creative reign, and grew as a woman with the company. I learned the value of teamwork, delegation, and the importance of allowing your team creative autonomy, which often led to unrelenting loyalty. I eventually worked up the nerve to turn in my resignation letter to Max and Lubov. I was a mess. The tears poured from my eyes with such fervor and force that you would have thought someone had died. My tears were tears of gratitude as I was grateful and moved beyond what words could express for Max, Lubov, Paula, and the entire BCBG community. I knew that because of my time there, I would be ready and equipped for whatever came my way.

> Because neither one of us wants to be the first to say goodbye.
> ~ expert from *Neither One of Us* by Gladys Knight and the Pips

Around 1999 there was a lot of buzz and momentum behind the "dot-com" industry. It was a train that mostly everyone was getting on. I was curious and interested in learning a new industry and figured I'd try my hand at it. With my years at BCBG, I knew I had a lot to offer any company. I was ready for a new challenge and the "dot-com" wave was it. In September 1999, I started working for modezone.com, an internet fashion company. I was hired on as the Vice President of Marketing with a six-figure salary. I was excited at the perks, benefits, and luxuries that the CEO lavished on employees. From leather décor in the lobby area, to expensive framed wall art, to top-of-the-line, executive-style desk chairs, this company spared no expense. From what I could tell the company was a profitable one and had the potential of being and having a major Internet presence. On top of that, the CEO held a Masters of Business Administration degree, which I was impressed by and we were about the same age. I had a GED and held in high regard any person with a professional degree. I just knew I would learn invaluable information about business management that my previous jobs had lacked in providing.

About three months into my new position, I started to notice that all wasn't thriving and well underneath the modezone.com surface. The CEO was more concerned with decorating the office than handling the day-to-day business operations. After a while, a clean-up guy was brought in to close out accounts and eventually shut the company down. I was allowed to work with the company until the very last day to assist the clean-up guy in closing out the accounts. Nine months into being there, the doors were closed and with it, my hopes of "making it" in the Internet business. As I saw it, the "dot-com" era had went "dot-gone" in less than a year. I was stumped: How could someone with a formal business education lack business "smarts" and on top of that, have no revenue stream? I was floored and could only shake my head at what I thought was a lack of common sense. I walked out of that office with a box of my belongings and three valuable lessons:

1. In order to run a successful company, money needed to come in before it went out.

2. Just because someone earned a MBA or other professional degree didn't mean they knew shit about business.

3. There was a change in the market as investors were looking to invest in tangible products, something they could touch, smell or even taste.

I went home that night to a full house. My dad was back around and I had my siblings with me. I went outside to take a breather. I ran my fingers through my hair and wondered how I was going to provide for myself and four other people. I had $6,000 to my name, which if not managed properly, could be spent in a month or two. I didn't know what to do. One thing was for certain: I had to do something.

What goes up must come down
Spinning wheel, got to go round
Talkin' bout your troubles
It's a crying sin
Ride a painted pony
let the spinning wheel spin.
~ excerpt from *Spinning Wheel* by Blood, Sweat & Tears

It was the 1980s and punk rock was the flavor of the decade. I was in my teens and was attending Fullerton High School in Fullerton, California. My mom had returned to styling hair and had taken on punk rock DJs, college guys, and musicians as clients. Since punk rock was about the attitude just as it was the music – and everyone was into it – we started to imitate the culture in our home. It became acceptable for my siblings and I to cuss and at times, it was actually celebrated. My mom's friends would come over and they'd party and smoke marijuana until the early morning hours. Rocky, who was about nine years old at the time, was given the task of "caring for the garden." We later discovered that the "garden" our mother kept referring to was a mini-marijuana garden. There was a constant stream of cocaine, drugs, beer, cigarettes, and other spirits in excess in our house more than there was food for us to eat. When mom was away, we'd scour the house looking for change so that we could buy milk, beans, and bread to

Me and my 80's
hair circa 1987

eat. Our mother had worked out deals with the attendants at the local liquor store, mini mart or gas station; she'd sell our food stamps to them in exchange for beer and cigarettes at about half the value. The worst part was that she would send us with a note to do the dirty deed for her.

We managed to get by finding money in hidden places in the apartment, but after a while even finding pennies became a challenge. We were upset, desperate, and hungry and had decided to walk up to the attendant to negotiate with him to stop accepting food stamps from our mother. When I shared our dilemma with the attendant, he gruffly responded, "Get out of here with that! Go home you kids!" He showed no sympathy and had not the slightest bit of remorse for his part in our situation. We left the store without the solution we had hoped for; however, we were determined to get even with the attendant. Once back at the house, Rocky came up with a plan for what would be the first of many of our "entrepreneurial endeavors." We went back to the store later in the week. Since I was the paranoid and "dramatic" one, I had to distract the manager or whoever was on duty. I spilled my slushie on the ground and started to cry. When the manager came over to check on me, Rocky and Angela filled up their backpacks and baseball hats with candy. Once they ran out of the store, I waited a few seconds then left the store without my slushie. We divided the candy and sold it at school the following day with huge markups. With the money, we were able to buy food and purchase basic necessities for the apartment. We continued this scheme, at different convenient stores in the neighborhood, until our Mom caught us. She had discovered our booty. To teach us a lesson, our mother tortured us daily by eating our profit away in front of us. She then called us "jackasses" for getting caught.

$6,000 AND A DREAM

Around this time, my mom started dating a Mexican guy from a rival neighborhood of my father's East L.A. hometown. I went ballistic. In my eyes, dating a rival was the ultimate betrayal to our father. I hadn't seen my dad since I left Arizona and had no way of getting in touch with him. I knew I had the upper hand because he was afraid of my family. I reminded him daily who my father was as he would lay on the couch – strung out on heroin with a gun on the coffee table – while my mom was at work. I verbally kicked him out of our house on many occasions, but he never listened. I threatened to slap the guy across the face with a tortilla if he didn't leave. "Do it," he challenged. And so I did. He sat there and did nothing in return.

Once my mom came home and heard what had happened, she became infuriated. This started the period of time where our mother resented and abused us. She often told us that she wished we were not there; however, she needed the money the state provided so she dealt with us. We were trapped in an environment that I wouldn't wish on any child. She started beating on Angela and I. For some reason, my mother and I did not see eye to eye and I became the object of her drunken fights. Angela would try to jump in and defend me, but we were often helpless against my mother. She was using cocaine, smoking marijuana, and drinking heavily, and anything we said or did had the potential of setting her off. If any of our friends had the required substances, she'd let them come hang out over our house. Our abode became the party house. She taught us how to play the "cocaine game." The game, contrary to its name, was innocent and wholesome. We would use her favorite "lady in red" mirrored picture frame as the base. One of us would get a cup and pack it with flour. We would then take turns slicing off a thin line until the mound crumbled. Whoever caused the mound to crumble was the loser.

One day, my mom had picked me up from my friend Jerine Voss's house. She showed up drunk and acted belligerently. She was irritable as we sat in the car driving to our apartment. I didn't say much and found it best to listen to her. I looked out the window as she rambled on to the left of me about any and everything that crossed her mind. Her voice became distant as I started to daydream. I watched as the buildings passed before me, becoming blurs in the side-view mirror. A few minutes later, she swerved and hit a curb. The tire blew out, which ticked her off even more. We made it to a gas station where the attendant proceeded to help us with the tire. My mom said something to me and I looked over at her. She grabbed my hair and slammed my head, face down, against the gear shifter. I heard her say something about me looking at her the wrong way. I was confused and my face stung from the impact. I put my hand on my lip; my palm was covered in blood. The gas attendant went inside and called the police on my mother. Once they arrived, the police talked with her and sent me home with her. She was obviously drunk and my face was busted and bloody, but they didn't intervene. The 80s was a different time and law enforcement didn't get involved as much in domestic issues. We made it back to our house on Truslow Street in Fullerton and she went inside. I started to walk down the street, with lip bleeding, back to the only place I felt safe, which was five miles away – my best friend Jerine's house.

After about four hours, I walked up and stopped in front of Jerine's driveway. From where I was standing, I could see her sitting at the table, eating with her family. Their family seemed so normal, picture perfect compared to mine. As I stood there watching them eat, Karol, Jerine's mom, spotted me. I saw the look of concern cross her face as she ran out of the dining room to the front door. The door opened and out came Jerine with her parents. "Tina, what happened to you?" Jerine asked in pure shock. I explained what happened as her parents escorted me into their house. I went to the bathroom and cleaned my face. Jerine's parents were in the other room talking. I saw Mr. Voss make a phone call. This wasn't the first time my mother had beaten me, and it wasn't the first time I sought refuge at Jerine's house. My mom was in the middle of a decade-long cocaine binge. Her mood was unpredictable and it was difficult to tell when she was OK or if she was going to flip out. I stayed over Jerine's house until the police came. My mother was with them. "I didn't beat her; she's such a drama queen," she said in response to police questioning. "She's always telling stories like that. She got out of hand and I had to be a parent." The police advised her to take me home and dismissed everything without further investigation. I refused to go. "She can stay with us, please," Karol Voss said to the officer. The officers and the Vosses looked at my mother. "Go ahead and keep that drama queen," my mom said. "I couldn't care less."

Karol and George Voss outside their family home, where I rented a room

Later that evening, Karol and George Voss came into Jerine's bedroom where we were preparing to go to sleep. "Tina, we have been talking," George said. "We are not rich but if you'd like, we would be willing to adopt you. You can live here but you'll have to find a way to pay rent. $150 a month." I looked at the both of them then looked at Jerine. I was given a chance to be in a safe and supportive environment for once. I happily accepted their offer. The Vosses, with the help of my principal at Fullerton High School who believed in my potential, helped me get my GED two years early, and they helped me go through the process of emancipation. When it came time for our hearing, my mom didn't show up (she had signed the papers beforehand though) so I was automatically granted emancipation from her. I secured a full-time job at Albertson's as a box girl to pay my rent. In more ways than one, the Voss family had changed my life; they probably saved it.

> She's got her ticket
> I think she gonna use it
> I think she going to fly away
> No one should try and stop her
> Persuade her with their power
> She says that her mind is made up.
> ~ excerpt from *She's Got Her Ticket* by Tracy Chapman

After leaving modezone.com I was determined to take my life into my hands. I was faced with a choice: either find a job working for someone else or carve out my own path. I needed the stability of a paycheck and even went out on a couple of job interviews. I was offered menial jobs, positions that were beneath my experience and pay grade. For instance, I interviewed for a position at Gap and felt I was qualified for a district manager position. Instead, they offered me an assistant manager position at one of their stores and sent me home with a Gap sweatshirt as a way to thank me for interviewing with them. I tossed it in the dumpster immediately. The freedom of calling my own shots fascinated and spoke to me more. I decided to take control of my professional life although I had no idea what I would do with it or where to even begin. Like my mom told me when I was younger: I was smart, I was pretty, and I could do what others did, but better. I knew I had what it took to be successful and leaned on her words for inspiration. My mom's words became my mantra, one that I held close by while navigating the trenches of uncertainty.

For six months, we lived on a shoe-string budget and only purchased the bare necessities. In our case, it was food – black beans, rice, and tortillas – and toiletries. I needed to get my dad back up and on his feet with work so that he could contribute around the apartment. I bought him a tool belt and a work van with the understanding that he'd support the house and stay clean and sober; no drugs, no alcohol. I was able to convince my landlord to hire my father as the handyman for the apartments he managed, and within a week, my dad was working. The money helped sustain us but was never quite enough to comfortably live off of. I ended up selling all of my jewelry, most painfully my vintage Rolex watch collection that I had collected the years I owned the vintage clothing stores, which helped to bring in some extra cash. We made it work, with tight budgeting and limited spending, I was able to make those dollars stretch. I still hadn't received any "aha" moments as to what I needed to do with a career but I knew without a doubt that something would come to me.

In December 2000, I received that moment of clarity that I had been praying and waiting on. I was on a date and had kicked off my shoes underneath the table. My date happened to look under the table and said in a disgusted tone, "Eww, what is that?" I looked under the table and saw that my insole had fallen out. I was beyond embarrassed and slid the insole back into my shoe. Later that evening, I started to go through my shoes. I picked one of the insoles up and watched as it wobbled back and forth in front of my face. I frowned at the bulk and shook my head at how unattractive that flimsy piece of material made my shoes look. With lightning speed, the thought hit me: I needed to create an insole that was comfortable and cute – a designer insole so to speak. Mostly all of the insole products were visually horrendous. I knew this as I had bought every kind during my BCBG and New York days. I went through all of my shoes and pulled out the insoles I had purchased for each pair. I dumped the insoles on the kitchen table creating a mountain of rubber foam madness and pulled out my notepad to do some sketches. My creative fire was lit and once I sat down and started doodling on my pad, I barely got up. I was like a mad scientist – completely engulfed in the project before me. I knew I had a kick-ass idea and I needed to move while my creative fire was hot.

> "Courage is the discovery that you may not win,
> and trying when you know you can lose,"
> – Tom Krause

Most of the insoles I had were over a year old so I knew I had to buy new ones to see if the design and look changed at all. As I went from shoe store to shoe department filling my basket with the various insoles, I noticed that they all looked the same. I became even more excited as I realized that no one was doing what I intended to do. The shoe accessories industry was in need of something fresh and chic, and I was just the person to give insoles a much-needed makeover. After purchasing every single pair of my "competitor's" products and researching the materials listed on the packaging, I made a key discovery. I noticed that each manufacturer used a portion of a material called PORON® in their insoles. I wasn't sure what PORON® was and hadn't the slightest idea on how it worked but I needed to find out. I didn't have a computer at home so I needed someone with Internet access to help me get the information I needed. I ended up calling my friend, Jen, at work and asked her to look up the manufacturer of PORON®. A few hours later, she called me back with a "1-800" number to the Rogers Corporation in Connecticut. It turned out PORON® is a shock-absorbing, durable foam urethane that is used in automobile bumpers and electronics. I had hit the jackpot and was eager to get on the phone with a company representative to share my idea and hear them say I was a genius. What I wasn't expecting was an automatic answering machine without an option for an operator. I was set back for all of one second before having the clever thought to make up extensions, which I did. After all I worked as a receptionist in my late teens. After about 20 tries, I connected with a gentleman named Roger, who happened to work in marketing. I was so happy to have finally gotten through to someone that I went straight into my idea after a very brief introduction. Thankfully, he did not think I was a nut job and actually liked my idea. He agreed to send me material samples and colors, and referred me to several converters. I sat there jotting down notes and stopped once he said converter. "Yes...of course...a converter," I said. I had no idea what he was talking about. "Umm...what exactly is a converter?" I asked. He chuckled then explained that their company sold raw materials only; a converter would take the raw materials and transform it into a finished product. He provided me with a list of three converters, all in the United States; I was adamant about manufacturing in the U.S., and wished me well on my venture.

I gave myself a couple minutes to digest everything before putting a call in to the converters. I was running off of adrenaline and didn't want to lose the momentum that I was gaining by the minute. I called two of the converters only to be brushed and cut off minutes into my spiel. On the last call, a woman answered the phone and listened to my idea with great interest. She was the assistant to the Vice President of Sales and agreed to have her boss call me back. She co-signed on my idea being "genius," which gave me even more of a push. An hour later, the vice president returned my call and we discussed the details. Once I had the

3R's Core Values: Resourcefulness

When making the decision to become an entrepreneur, sometimes the hardest step to take is actually the first one, which is to start. You don't need to know everything, have all of your 'ducks in a row' or know exactly where you're going to get started. Just start! Use what you have at that moment, which may be nothing more than a pen/pencil and a sheet of paper. Use that and ponder the following questions: What can you do to get started? Where can you find resources? How can you create the little successes that will lead to the bigger successes? Hopes and dreams are not enough for entrepreneurs; you will need a solid plan. So start by writing it down!

specifications and design nailed down, they would make me some samples. I had to come up with $1,500 to cover the tooling fee and send them a sketch of the designs. Once Roger sent me the sample PORON® material, I cut, glued, and taped the pieces together so that it resembled the sketch I drew out. And yes, I used duct tape. I guess my dad was right!

Creatively, I was at an all-time high and my life had taken on a new direction. We were poor with barely a few hundred dollars between us, but the excitement of what I was creating trumped any fears and lack of experience. My family was supportive, was there to listen to my ideas, and gave me a fresh perspective on the direction I could take my project. There were plenty of nights where my dad and I would sit at the kitchen table and drink coffee as I scribbled away in my notepad. It reminded me of my childhood, and was a sweet visit from my past that I welcomed and needed. While my dad provided insight on the product measurements and dimensions, my mom helped me design the packaging. I drove down to her apartment one night and shared with her what I was doing. We pulled a couple of chairs up to the table, smoked a joint, and drank Corona beer with limes, then started to draw package concepts. That same night, the name and tagline was born: *Foot Petals. For those of us who have a love/hate relationship with our sexy shoes*. In Phylis fashion, my mom told me not to quit my day job. When I reminded her that I didn't have one, she quipped, "Maybe you should think about getting one." We laughed it off and spent that night joking and laughing. I woke up the next day with a hangover from drinking one too many Coronas with my mom. I decided to go home with my little project in hand. I realized my mom was better at being more of a friend than a "traditional mother."

You just call out my name
And you know wherever I am
I'll come running to see you again
~ excerpt from *You've Got a Friend* by Carole King

Me and Margie, 2011

CHAPTER FOUR

Angel of Mine

My Frankenstein-like prototype had become a permanent accessory as I carried it with me everywhere I went. All I needed was the $1,500 to finally move forward on getting the product samples created. Since I didn't have the money, the prototype had to do. It served as a sample for others and a visual representation and motivation of my dream. I was itching to share what I had with friends, but wanted and needed something a bit more professional than the duct-taped and glued sample I put together. The prototype worked though and the few people I shared it with could see past its physical appearance to the bigger vision I had in mind.

In the early months of 2001, Margie came out from New York to Los Angeles on a business trip. She was working for Michael Stars, the hottest T-shirt company at the time, and was the head of their national sales division. I had mentioned my idea to her several times during our phone conversations, and with her in Los Angeles, I was finally able to show her the prototype. While she looked the prototype over, turning it to get a sense and feel of it, I asked her if I made it, would she be able to sell it. In my mind, Margie was the best; she was a sales guru. I knew if placed in her hands, *Foot Petals* would blossom. She didn't answer right away and instead took the prototype back to New York with her to shop around to some friends and industry people. Within a week or two, she called me up. Before I could ask how she was doing, Margie excitedly said, "I think we really have something here!" Margie's stamp of approval was the green light I needed. We started to set our sights on securing an investor.

Although the "dot-com" industry went bust, I had access to a few of the venture capitalists who had invested in modezone.com. I figured since they lost a lot of money in the Internet business that they would be interested in investing in an actual "tangible product." I started to probe and ask my friends for potential leads on investors. My good friend JJ, who I met when we were 15 years old, had a father-in-law who was an investor known to invest in Latino businesses. JJ scheduled a lunch meeting with me and Mr. Armando DuPont and I had a week to create a presentation. I had learned how to present in front of a board of directors while at modezone.com and felt confident that I would nail the presentation. I wasn't as confident on the content of the presentation as I didn't know a thing about a business plan, let alone how to write one. I researched different business plans and created a presentation with the little I knew. When I met with Mr. DuPont and his wife for lunch, my passion for the product took over and I was able to clearly convey my vision, goals, and the necessity for *Foot Petals*. Mr. DuPont had never invested in a Latina company before, but when he pulled out his checkbook after my presentation and wrote me a check for $10,000, I had become the first one. I had never received a check for that amount before in my life and felt as if I hit the lotto. Mr. DuPont became my angel investor and business partner that day, and provided me the financial backing and business know-how to get the ball rolling.

Tina's Tip

You determine how much someone else will believe in your dream. People will invest in you when they see you are willing to invest in yourself.

3M's Best Practice: Money

When starting a new business, it is typical and quite normal for entrepreneurs to struggle with capital and start-up costs. Some people tap into their savings and earnings to help offset costs, but for most, even that is not a viable option. An entrepreneur can curb some of the earlier expenses by bartering for services, employing interns to handle certain tasks, and/or seeking sponsors and investors to name a few ideas. Before courting an investor, be sure to consider the following questions: How much money do I need? How will I manage this money? What and when is the return on investment?

ANGEL OF MINE

I left my meeting with Mr. DuPont feeling very inspired and ready to make moves. I deposited the check and placed the order for the samples with the converter as soon as I made it home. I then called a long-time business associate, a printer, who I had developed a relationship with when I worked at BCBG and had tremendous respect for. I knew that with my samples ordered, I would need packaging and marketing materials. He agreed to help me with my printing needs. The only thing I could give him in exchange was my word that I would eventually pay him back. I was worried as I didn't know when that would be or how long it would take. He quelled my fears when he said, "Tina, I know that you will pay me; I trust you. Don't worry about it." I was starting to see some light at the end of the tunnel. My dreams of someday "making it" were finally starting to take form.

Dream on
Dream on
Dream on
Dream until the dream come true.
~ excerpt from *Dream On* by Aerosmith

It was the summer of 1978 and I was going into my fourth grade year of school. I was at the beach with my family, running barefoot in the sand. My aunt was a few steps ahead of me as I trailed behind trying to catch her. She looked back at me, smiled, and then continued to run a bit faster. Suddenly, she fell to the ground, rolled over, and grabbed her left foot. She started to yell out and I could tell she was in pain. I kept running and stopped on the spot where my aunt fell. There was an intense burning sensation on the bottom of my feet and I started to smell something similar to burnt flesh. I fell over and grabbed my feet. My soles felt like they were on fire. I started to cry and continued to hold my feet. My aunt and I had run over hot coals that had been buried under the sand.

My family rushed us to the hospital but none of the hospitals in Los Angeles were equipped to deal with burns. They ended up taking me to the only burn center in the country at the time, which was at the University of California-Irvine in Orange County. I had extreme third-degree burns on my feet and had to stay in the hospital for weeks. I was confined to a wheelchair for nearly six months and eventually used crutches to walk around with. My aunt had suffered third-degree burns on her left foot, and had to use crutches and a wheelchair as well. Since I was in physical therapy in Orange County, my family eventually relocated to Orange County so that they could get me to my appointments with ease and on time. The daily commute from Los Angeles to Orange County had become taxing on my family and the move helped alleviate that drive. I remained in therapy for an additional three months and with time it became easier to walk around without the assistance of my crutches. Although the skin on my feet had replaced itself and the soles were at least 95 percent healed, my feet remained sensitive to the touch from that point on.

Through the fire,
through whatever come what may.
~ excerpt from *Through the Fire* by Chaka Khan

With the initial investment made and the orders for the product placed, I did an initial run of 2,500 units; it was cheaper to order in large quantities, my dream of doing something big had started to materialize. The $10,000 was gone and there was still so much more left to do. I had to secure a graphic designer to design the logo and artwork for packaging and promotional materials, in addition to trademarking the name "Foot Petals," registering with the United Code Council to obtain Universal Product Codes (UPCs), creating line sheets and wholesale sets for buyers to buy the product in bulk, and securing a distribution center that could warehouse and distribute our products. I learned the art of using my resources and bartering, and wasn't afraid to offer those I worked with and developed a relationship with a percentage of the company. I offered the graphic designer five percent ownership of the company since I couldn't afford to pay her at the time I used her services. Our agreement was working out fine until her boyfriend stepped in and demanded that she ask for payment for her services upfront. I couldn't convince her to accept my offer for partial ownership in the company and had to scramble to pay her

Me and Angela working a festival in California

$10,000 for her work. Sadly, we never spoke again after that. I often wonder if she is still with her boyfriend. I mean let's face it, the guy gypped her out of over half a million dollars in the long run.

Foot Petals may not have been much at the time, but I knew it was going to grow into something big. My excitement and passion about my product was infectious; as I explained what I was doing, more and more people were willing to come on board and help me achieve my goals. This excitement bubbled over into the apartment, which doubled as a living space for my father, two younger brothers, and I, and as an office space for the company. A week after the initial investment, my dad made and installed custom shelves and drawers for the products, with the prototype being the first thing we placed on it. I was happy and excited for everything that was in store and glad to have the support of my family.

Within a month, the graphics for the packaging were complete. I turned the files over to Sam, my printer, and he started to prepare for the initial print run. I went down to his office to look over the proofs. I paid close attention to the placement, spelling, colors, everything. I was about to give Sam the go ahead when I had a thought: *Foot Petals* was not going to be the only product I created. I stood there for a second then realized it would be better, and smarter, to name the brand *Foot Petals* as opposed to the insole itself. I was stumped. If *Foot Petals* was to be the name of the company, then what would I call the product? I walked up and down the office, wracking my brain on a name. Sam stood beside me and helped out as best he could with suggestions but nothing stuck. "What do these things do?" I said still pacing the room. "What do they protect?" By this point, I was walking across the office on my tip toes as if wearing high-heeled shoes. "Tip Toes!" I exclaimed. "I'll call it *Tip Toes*!" The insole was a flower-shaped cushion that fit on to the ball and toe area of high heels, which was where most of the pressure went when wearing heels. It only made sense to call it *Tip Toes*. Sam prompted me to make the changes to the file with the art department. I ran to the back and shared the changes with them. Twenty minutes later, new proofs were printed with the corrections. I signed off on the prints. Sam gave the printers the approval to start making the packaging. I walked out of there with the new name of my company, *Foot Petals*, the company's first product, *Tip Toes*, and a $113,500.61 balance.

Once the packaging was ready, the apartment became a makeshift and temporary distribution center. Since I didn't have a warehouse to store the product and packaging, the apartment had to do. We had our own assembly line of workers: my father, Richard, Kady, Eric, Angela and her daughter Jaz (they lived a few streets over from me), and me. The kids would help put the packaging together at night and would often go to school with paper cuts on their fingers the next day. They never complained, except for when we went to the store and they wanted something I couldn't afford to buy at the time, like toys. Richard was 10, Kady was seven, and Eric was five and they all were into collecting Pokemon cards. After turning down their requests for the cards for the umpteenth time, I took them home and sat with them at the kitchen table. I handed Kady the calculator and gave Eric the bills to open. Richard would read off how much each bill cost. We created a budget together which helped them to understand money and gave them a clearer perspective on why I wasn't able to always buy what they wanted. They learned the lesson and were even more appreciative when I did surprise them with toys. Creating a budget for the checkbook and paying the bills became our monthly ritual.

Tina's Tip

Good can, and often times will, come out of a seemingly 'bad' situation. Refrain from judging as much as possible; you might be pleasantly surprised.

Give me a nickel
brother can you spare a dime
Money can drive some people out of their minds.
~ excerpt from *For the Love of Money* by The O'Jays

It was time to start getting a return on our investment and to see if the market was ready for our product. With Margie in New York heading up sales for the company, she was able to keep an eye and ear out for possible locations and events to introduce our product. Margie had worked her magic and secured us a booth at ENK International, one of the most renowned and respected trade shows in the fashion world. The show was in August 2001 and booth spaces had been sold out for at least a year. After putting in a call to the coordinator of the event and pulling a few strings, Margie got us a spot at the show within two weeks of the event. With less than $500 in my bank account, I bought a round trip ticket to New York. ENK International would be a make or break moment for us. We would have to convince people to actually buy the product. We knew what was ahead of us and were well aware of the doors a successful show would open for us.

I arrived in New York the night before the show started and stayed with Margie. It felt good to see her and I was happy to have her embarking on this new venture with me. We arrived at the Javits Center the next morning, the first day of the show. We each grabbed boxes and headed inside to find our point of contact. We reached the registration table and after checking in, were escorted to our location. We walked past the booths of new and upcoming fashion designers such as *Me and Ro*, *Lucky Brand*, and *Le Sport Sac*. We continued walking until Maria, the coordinator, stopped. "The location is not very appealing," she said, pointing to a table wedged between the entrance to the MEN'S and WOMEN'S RESTROOMS. "We basically had to create a last-minute space for you. You have 30 minutes to set up your booth. Good luck, ladies." I was speechless and turned to look at Margie. I was about to cry. "It's perfect – absolutely perfect," Margie said. "In order for them to do their business in there, they will have to pass us first." I loosened up a bit and figured she had a point. We set up our booth and waited for the crowd to come in.

It was well into the morning and no one showed interest in stopping at our booth. Several people flowed in and out of the bathroom, but they all avoided eye contact with us. After hours of sitting behind our booth, Margie suddenly ran in front of the booth and stopped a female buyer. "What is more valuable than air?" Margie asked her. "My time," the woman curtly responded. Margie, standing in front of the woman, handed her a *Tip Toe*. "Everybody's got to walk, right?" Margie asked the woman. "Just put one in your right shoe to try it out." The woman looked skeptical. "If it doesn't work, you can come back and bite my head off." The woman took the sample from Margie and hurriedly walked off. By this time, a few buyers had started to slow down to see what the commotion was about. We had a small window of opportunity to draw in buyers, so Margie and I jumped into our show.

"Hey Tina," Margie said.

"Yes Margie," I responded.

"How much do you believe in this product?" Margie asked.

"I'll tell you what Margie, if *Foot Petals* doesn't bring comfort to your feet, I'll give you a pair for free," I said. More and more people started to come to our booth and before we knew it, we had a crowd. We passed out one sample and encouraged buyers to try them out as they walked around the trade show. If they were satisfied, we encouraged them to come back to the booth to get the other half of the pair.

It didn't take long before buyers returned to our booth requesting the other half of the pair of *Tip Toes* insoles. One of the buyers was so impressed that the insoles "actually worked" that she signed a purchase order on behalf of her company – Andersons Bride in Alaska. The second person to sign a purchase order was the buyer for Patricia Fields, costume designer for the popular television series *Sex and the City*. "Do you know how many stilettos we go through every episode?" she asked. "We need to get a bunch of these." The interest in our product continued to build as celebrities, high-profile buyers, and more came by our booth to either get a sample and/or sign a purchase sheet. We were winning. Each time a purchase order was signed, our excitement only grew. By the end of the day, we had secured 250 orders totaling $50,000. Margie and I were ecstatic and couldn't believe how our little space between the bathrooms actually paid off. We were experiencing a natural high and knew that things were only going to get better.

FROM STILETTOS TO THE STOCK EXCHANGE

"Keep away from those who try to belittle
your ambitions. Small people always do
that, but the really great make you believe
that you too can become great."
– Mark Twain

Me and Margie at our first trade show, ENK in New York City

Me and Jen working a pre-Emmy's style lounge in Beverly Hills

CHAPTER FIVE

Making Room For Growth

I couldn't believe Margie and I left the Javits Center with $50,000 in purchase orders. I had this overwhelming feeling of happiness and a bit of anxiety take over me as I realized what had happened. We proved that *Foot Petals* was a viable brand, one that people needed and wanted. We had introduced the product to the market and the market (a representation of it at least) responded favorably. I knew from the beginning that this product was a great idea and after the trade show, everyone else knew too. I could not wait to return home as I had to place an order with Remington, the factory in Ohio, for the cushions and with Sam for packaging. We had our work cut out for us. I knew the orders would only continue to come in especially as more people learned of the product and as existing customers placed new orders. As the plane approached Los Angeles, I remembered that I had other business to tend to as well: Family business.

Two weeks before I flew to New York for ENK International, I had walked over to Richard and Eric's school so that I could walk back home with them. Kady was staying with Angela during this time. They both ran over to where I was standing and we started walking back towards our Santa Monica apartment. Eric was in the thick of his story, giving details on his day, what they did in class, and what he learned. He dominated the conversation so much that it took me a minute to realize that Richard hadn't said anything. "Is everything OK?" I asked Richard. He didn't respond with a verbal answer and instead shrugged his shoulders. "He's mad," Eric said matter-of-factly. "Shut up!" Richard snapped. I figured something must have happened at school. "Mad...why, what's wrong?" I probed.

"He's mad because dad is drinking and sticking needles in his arm again when you're not at home," Eric said. "Shut up!" Richard repeated. I stopped and asked Richard how long this had been going on. Eric kept talking and Richard kept telling him to "shut up" and eventually called him a "rat bastard." I quickly ended the argument that had started between them. After they both calmed down, I had learned that my dad invited his friends over to the house where they'd drink and do heroin while I was away. I also found out that he would sometimes drive around drunk with my two brothers. This concerned me more than anything as he had not only placed his life in danger, but the lives of my younger brothers as well. Our agreement was that in order for him to stay at the apartment that he had to remain clean and sober (no drugs, no alcohol) and that he had to work. I was devastated. Things were seemingly good with us and I had no way of knowing what he was up to when I wasn't around. I told the boys not to worry about anything and that I'd take care of it. I didn't know how to approach the situation, but I knew that I would and I had to.

About a week after my talk with Richard and Eric, I ran into my landlord as I walked into my apartment. A part of me felt like he was watching and waiting for me to come home. The way he sprung out from the bushes like a ninja startled me. "Tina, we need to talk," the landlord said. Those were the four words I hated to hear. "What can I do for you?" I asked. "Your father is out of control; he is threatening tenants. When you're gone he has his thug friends here doing drugs."

"I'm so sorry," I said, embarrassed.
"He can't work here anymore. I spoke with the company. If his friends show up again, I'm calling the cops and you'll have to move out," he said.
I apologized again and assured him that I would handle everything upon my return from New York. I was so disappointed and upset with my father. I got my dad that job and it only took him a few months to mess it all up.

"Insanity is doing the same thing over and over again but expecting different results."
– Albert Einstein

Dad flippin' the bird

I arrived at the airport a bit exhausted yet ready to get my house in order. I hadn't figured out how I would approach my father but I knew I had to handle it that night. I waited for about 15 minutes before my dad pulled up. He jumped out of the car, grabbed my bags, and gave me a hug. He was happy to see me. I got in the car and noticed several empty beer cans on the floor. There was a freshly opened can of beer in the driver's side cup holder. I moved the beer over to the passenger side cup holder and drove home.

We reached the apartment and as soon as I opened the door, I knew our conversation would be a hard one to have. While I was gone, my father had shined and lined my stilettos along the hallway wall, folded the laundry, cleaned the apartment, and installed more shelves and drawers. My dad always took care of me. He always found a way to make sure I was OK. Even as a child, I was very tender-headed. My dad would do my hair whenever my mom's combing and brushing was too much for my head to take. I was definitely daddy's little princess. "Mija, look what I did," my dad said and pointed to the new shelves. "I made you new shelves." I took a deep breath. I don't remember thanking him. "Did you make those drawers before or after you and your friends got wasted in my home?" I asked. My dad immediately became defensive. "What the fuck are you screaming at me for? Look I take care of the place," he said. I told him about my conversation with the landlord and that I knew he was drinking and driving while the kids were with him. By this time, my brothers stood in the hallway. They were silent as my dad and I argued back and forth. He wouldn't admit to any wrongdoing and insisted that I calm down. I was heated and wanted nothing more than for him to understand where I was coming from. He instead walked into one of the bedrooms and came out with two bags. "Come on boys, let's go," he said to Richard and Eric. He knew exactly how to get to me: through my siblings. "No… wait," I said.

"Let's go," he yelled out as Eric reached for his hand. Richard stood still.
"I'm not going, dad," he said.
"You're not staying here!" my dad insisted.
"Mijo, you can stay with me," I said to Richard.
"No, I don't like it here. You're too strict," he said. "I want to go live with my mom."

Me, Richard and Eric - Our first year living together

I felt the tears run down my cheeks as I explained to Richard that he couldn't live with his mom until she stopped using drugs and had a place to live. He insisted that he didn't want to live in a van with our father or stay with me.

"I'll go into foster care," he eventually said. "Tina, will you call for me?" I was exhausted and felt the bit of progress I made in New York crumble at my feet.

"Fuck you and fuck you," my dad said to me and Richard. He stormed out of the apartment with Eric and drove off in the work van I had bought him.

I was hurt and worried for the well-being of my dad and Eric. I relegated myself to the apartment for a few days and drove around to see if I could locate them. Richard moved in with his friend's family and remained there for about eight months. He eventually went back to live with his mother until child services was called. He was taken into foster care. I wanted him to come live with me but he chose foster care instead. I was disheveled but had to get my thoughts and my life back in order. Although things were falling apart with my family, I still had to tend to and nurture *Foot Petals*. I had to brush myself off and get back into the swing of things business-wise. I put a call in to the factory to cover the purchase orders then called Sam to place an additional order for packaging. As I delved more into the company, I was able to distract myself from worrying too much about my dad and brothers. I had to trust that everything happened the way it was supposed to when it was supposed to. This was hard for my heart to comprehend, but with my mind on my company, trusting in the process was something that became easier to do day by day.

A couple of weeks passed and I was able to get completely focused on *Foot Petals*. My friend Jen – who helped me research the material PORON® when I first had the idea to create an insole – was about to launch her public relations company. Her lease was up on her apartment and she needed to find another place to live. I saw an opportunity and offered Jen to stay with me, rent free, in exchange for being her first client. She happily accepted. Jen moved in shortly after my father and the boys moved out. We were halfway into production and were itching to get the orders into the buyers' hands. I had set up meetings with local retailers to shop our product and had made headway in building support locally. I woke up early this one particular Tuesday as I had a few meetings scheduled in Los Angeles. Jen turned the TV on the news station so that we could listen as I got ready in my bedroom. I overheard the newscasters say something about the World Trade Centers, planes, and terrorism so I walked into the living room to see what was going on. Smoke, dust, and debris filled the screen as the anchorman reported live from NYC. We couldn't believe what we saw; I sat on the arm of my couch to stabilize myself. People were in the streets, covered in soot, the images of the Twin Towers falling one after the other looped in the top left corner of the screen. I struggled with accepting what flashed before my eyes as it seemed like something out of a movie. I sat there dazed for a few minutes before I screamed out, "Margie!" I panicked as my best friend was in New York while the attacks were happening and I needed to know that she was OK. I called her cell phone; no response. I hung up then immediately called her house phone.

"Hello?" she answered frantically.

"Margie, oh my gosh…are you OK?" I asked.

"Wha-what's going on?" she asked. "I have no idea what's going on…we don't have any reception out here."

I explained what happened and shared information with her as it was reported. We both cried and held the phone in utter shock and disbelief. We stayed on the line for a few before Margie got off. She promised to call back. I sat there for a few minutes more then realized that Jen and I had meetings to get to. We got in my car and headed towards downtown Los Angeles. I turned on the radio and we listened in as disc jockeys advised to stay out of downtown. Traffic was backed up and the police had blocked off certain streets that led into downtown. The city was on high alert; since LA was a major city, there was concern and much speculation that a similar attack would take place there. I turned the car around and we headed home. I called my appointments only to find out that meetings were cancelled for the day. It was one of those moments where I wanted to be with my family.

> "All endings are also beginnings.
> We just don't know it at the time."
> – Mitch Albam

BUMPY DAYS AHEAD

The panic that filled the air was thick and heavy. No one knew what to do and fear had gripped the nation in a way most hadn't experienced in their lifetimes. The days after the attack, I went out to stock up on water and nonperishable food in case a similar attack happened in California as so many had suspected. Thankfully, the city was not targeted and as the days passed, people returned to their routine. I flew out to Chicago for another trade show days after the attack. Margie was stuck in New York and was unable to meet Jen and I there. Neither of us wanted to go but our plane tickets were purchased and we had paid for booth space. We flew to Chicago and hopped on a taxi to McCormick Convention Center in downtown Chicago. As the taxi pulled off, I noticed how desolate McCormick Place looked. I walked to the door, rolling my sample boxes and presentation materials behind me, and stepped inside. There wasn't a single soul in the building. "Hello?" I said. There was no response. We walked around to see if we could find someone to talk to, but no one was there. There we were with product in hand and no one to show it to. We caught a taxi back to the airport; all we wanted to do was get home.

Twelve hours and a layover later, I was back in the comfort of my home. I looked at my answering machine. I had about 15 messages, which was new, as I had never received that many messages in such a short amount of time. "Hi…this is Carol from Macy's. Because of the recent attacks, we have to cancel all orders made in the past 60 days…I'm so sorry." That was the first message and there were 12 other messages similar to it. I started to freak out and wanted to curse every and anything in sight. We were halfway into production; there was no way we could cancel that order. As far as I was concerned, we were screwed. "Tina, don't freak out." I heard a familiar voice say. Margie had left me a voice message; she knew me so well. I called her and she answered right away. "Margie, at least 14 buyers have called in to cancel their orders," I fumed.

"What are we going to do now?! We are fucked!"

"Tina, calm down," Margie said. "Look, I've been getting calls all day too. People are pulling out because they are scared but we are going to be OK."

I didn't see how we were going to survive such a hit. We were in production for $50,000 worth of purchase orders that were being cancelled by the day, which meant we wouldn't have the money to pay the factory. I was beyond freaked out. I wanted to disappear.

"Look, most of those orders were from big names and retailers. We are going to have to go after smaller buyers and retailers," she assured. "We are going to be OK." I wasn't totally convinced but at that point, I had no other choice.

In the weeks that followed, we reached out to and cultivated new relationships, and secured new purchase orders. I went door to door in various retail communities in southern California and shopped the product while Margie worked her contacts in New York. Between the two of us, we were able to cover most of the cancelled purchase orders. Once the cushions and packaging shipped to the office, a.k.a. my apartment, we started packing and preparing the cushions for shipment. Two weeks later, all orders were processed and shipped. I had the paper cuts to prove it.

We continued to meet with new buyers and scheduled presentations with interested independent retailers. I had wrapped a meeting with a buyer when I received a call from a local number. I figured it was another potential buyer. I was wrong.

"Hello?"
"Miss Aldatz? Hi, this is Officer Blake from the Santa Monica Police Department."
"Yes?" I said in a nervous tone. I didn't know what he was going to tell me but a part of me felt that it had something to do with my dad and brothers. "We are at your place of residence. There was a break-in," he said.

I stood there in silence and listened as he explained what he believed had happened. I got in my car and drove home. Once there, Officer Blake explained in detail that a neighbor reported "an Hispanic male, about 5'9" standing outside a white van earlier in the morning" and that a "little boy" entered the apartment through the side window. I sighed. I knew who fit those descriptions. "They weren't sure but they said it may have been a family member," he continued.

"No, my family is out of town," I said. I was tired and didn't feel like dealing with the situation any further. "We'd like to know if you can identify any stolen items. Let's go through and take a look," he suggested.

"No. Look officer, it's OK," I said. "I'll figure it out."

He asked me if I was sure and I told him I was; I thanked him for calling and went inside. I walked room to room and nothing was out of place. I went into my bedroom and opened my jewelry box; it was empty. My diamonds, necklaces, earrings, everything was missing. "Damn," I said aloud. Thankfully, none of Jen's belongings were missing.

After a few days, I figured out what happened. I received a phone call from the owner of one of the pawn shops in the city who got my number from my Aunt Lonnie. He called my aunt to tell her that my dad had pawned diamonds and suspected that he wasn't up to any good. My Aunt Lonnie told me what happened and after I spoke to the owner of the pawn shop, I drove over to retrieve my jewelry. I had to pay money that I didn't necessarily have at the time to get my diamonds back. I was infuriated and hurt. As much as I loved my dad, I had to distance myself from him. I wanted to go after him, to beg him and Eric to stay with me, but it would have been pointless. My dad was using and selling heroin and drinking incessantly; there was no way I would be able to get through to him. I continued to focus my energy on building the company and prayed that God would keep my family safe and protected.

CHAPTER SIX
All On The Line

Towards the end of 2001, Armando sent an accountant to my apartment to help set up the company's infrastructure. Money was extremely tight and we were often late in paying our suppliers. The factory extended us some credit since Armando had cash, but there was a lot of money that needed to exchange hands. We didn't factor in how much time it would take us to receive payment from the retailers. It took eight weeks to make the product, package it, bundle it and ship it. In order to work with the buyers, we had to extend "Net 30" terms, which meant the buyers would send in payment 30 days after receiving the product. With this set-up, it took us on average about 120 days to receive payment on the orders. Most times, we had to chase down the buyers to get our money as most of them did not remit payment after the 30 days had lapsed. In order to grow we needed to have a better system in place, which is where Pat the accountant came in.

As a creative, I admittedly knew very little about infrastructure, accounting, and other business terms, and was very unhappy with Pat around. I felt creatively stifled as day by day, month by month, I had to listen to and answer questions for this hard-nosed, no-nonsense woman. She wanted to know every detail, and only seemed to care about how every single penny was allocated. I was frustrated and grew resentful as I felt the fun was being zapped out of the company. I was vocal in sharing my disdain with Armando and I'm sure I wasn't Pat's favorite client. I kicked, screamed, and complained the entire time she was there, which was about two years to be exact. I wanted to do what I did best, which was to create and come up with cool and out-of-the-box ideas and concepts for public relations, marketing, and advertising campaigns. With Pat around, I was reminded daily of what I could and could not do financially, which lowered my spirits and nearly killed my dreams. I had all of this creative energy bubbling inside of me that I had to contain because most of what I had in mind – a $3-5 million ad campaign – wasn't in the best interest financially for the company. I was bummed.

As the adage goes, necessity is the mother of invention. Once I realized that my million-dollar ad campaign wouldn't be approved, Jen and I focused even more on getting *Foot Petals* placement in magazines and TV spots. Our first order of business was to get the product in magazines and other national publications. We realized a good review on our product was worth more value than a glossy photo spread of the product in which no one would know if the product worked or not. We compiled a list of publications and researched the contacts for each magazine's editorial team. The first publication we sent *Foot Petals* to was *SELF* magazine. We were excited and pumped, and couldn't wait to hear back from the magazine regarding our product. About a month after sending a sample and press kit, we received a letter from the editor that they had accepted the sample and would review it for a month. We were thrilled and equally nervous. Although we made it to the review and would have a write-up in the magazine,

Filming a segment with American Express

we wouldn't know how they graded the product until the publication hit the newsstands. We would find out what they thought about *Foot Petals* when everyone else did. That was a bit nerve-wrecking but we had more than enough work to keep us busy and our minds off what they thought about us.

Every day was a waiting game but we played it well. We continued to go to meetings, make phone calls with potential buyers, and build our public relations strategy. As much as I tried to divert my attention, I was on pins and needles about the review.

3M's Best Practice: Marketing

Branding and promotion is the lifeblood of every successful business. You can have an amazing service or product, but if no one is aware of what you have to offer, then you might as well not have an amazing service or product at all. When looking at the best and most effective ways to market your brand, consider the following questions: Who is my customer? How are they going to hear about the product? What's going to drive them to action, or what is going to compel them to buy my product and/or service? Then set out to put a plan in action that will promote and position your products and/or services in the market.

That whole words will never hurt me thing wasn't completely true. In our situation, words – positive or negative – would leave more of an impact/damage to our brand than mere sticks and stones. We could bounce back from sticks and stones, but a bad review? Not so much. Our moment came when in June 2002, I received a call from the Editor-At-Large of SELF magazine. The review was in the June issue of the magazine. It was pretty early in the morning when we got the call, so Jen and I threw on some clothes and headed to the nearest newsstand. We spotted a stand and jumped out of the car. We opened the magazine and flipped through the pages. We found the article and screamed: We were rated 'Grade A' by the SELF magazine editors. We bought a few copies then headed back to the apartment. I called Margie and we all screamed and relished in our first magazine placement.

The review put us on the map and within hours, our phone lines were ringing with new buyers and customers who read the article. We knew a good review would open doors for the company but we weren't expecting it to happen all on the same day. We were so excited that later in the day after we finished up with calls and e-mails, Jen and I drove to Venice Beach to get tattoos. Jen got a tattoo of a red chili pepper; I got a tattoo of a woman emerging from a chrysalis, which represented the program my mom went through while at the women's shelter. It was a reminder for me to never forget where I'd come from. We left the parlor and went to a local Mexican Cantina where we celebrated over Bloody Mary's, margaritas, and fajitas. Our hard work had started to pay off but we were well aware that there was still more work to be done.

Oh I'm out here trying to make it,
baby can't you see It takes a lot of money
to make it let's talk truthfully
So keep your love light burning
And a little food hot in my plate
You might as well get used to me
coming home a little late
~ excerpt from *Work to Do* by The Isley Brothers

LEARNING YOUR LIMITS

We continued to make strides with *Foot Petals* and watched the brand grow in popularity. We were still under Pat's eagle eye and had to continue to network, barter, and use our resources in order to build momentum around the company's public relations and marketing. It helped that celebrities such as Rachel Zoe sung our praises, which alone helped us garner name recognition, but it wasn't enough. I had a good friend, Mistala, from back in my South Coast Plaza Victoria's Secret days. She now worked at the ABC network in production. ABC had a segment that ran on Fridays, *Freebie Fridays*, where viewers would call in and comment on the featured product. We were able to get *Tip Toes* on the show and gave out samples to over 100 viewers. When the segment aired with our product, we received positive feedback from callers and viewers who had tested and tried the products out for themselves. This helped us build a grassroots marketing presence and created another outlet to increase brand exposure. I also saw the necessity of cultivating relationships with people. We were able to get *Foot Petals* off the ground because of the support of friends and former co-workers who believed in the company. They were just as excited and invested in its success as I was.

As the orders from independent retailers grew, the size of our company grew too. I hired Angela to come on board as a sales representative. Our office was still in my apartment and with my sister as an employee we needed to move to a bigger space. I found a 750-square foot office space in Culver City, California, and rented it out. It was our first official *Foot Petals* office. I hired an office manager within a few weeks of being at our new office, and together our four-member team set out to take over the shoe accessories industry. The office was small but it was quite efficient and helped us get the job done. We were inspired and the move to a new space helped us recharge and refuel our creativity. I came up with a new product that would protect the backs of women's heels when wearing pumps, *Heavenly Heels*. With two products to offer, the company had become even more marketable which would increase and diversify our orders. After fighting against Pat's suggestions, I finally started to understand her methods and approach to finances. I started to review the monthly financial reports and became interested in what it meant and how it worked. I learned the importance of having revenue coming in versus revenue going out. Up until that point, I only saw the company from the creative perspective: brainstorming ideas, creating a product, printing samples, production, marketing and design. I did not realize that even those aspects contributed to the bottom line and had to be accounted for. I started to become more knowledgeable in business, which helped me become a better businesswoman.

Tina's Tip

It's always good to know how to do a little bit of everything. However, do not be afraid to hire or bring on the professionals to do what you are not skilled or do not have the time to do.

3M's Best Practice: Marketing

A business is only as strong as its infrastructure! When starting a new company, it may be easy – and almost second nature – to overlook the mundane tasks of accounting, legal paperwork, strategic growth plans, etc. for the more fun tasks such as product creation, marketing and advertising campaigns. In order to do what I love – which is to create products – I needed to have a solid infrastructure – the systems and processes that make the business possible – in place. The infrastructure is the foundation that allows and positions the business for growth; it is what gives you the freedom to create more!

With a three-woman sales team that consisted of Margie, Angela and me, we were able to attend and participate in more trade shows. We would have several buyers at a time come by to check out our products and it always felt good when they expressed their interest or satisfaction. On one occasion, a buyer had picked up the cushion and looked it over as I explained how the product worked. As I wrapped up my pitch, the buyer threw the cushion at the table then said, "I could buy these things for a dollar." I became so upset and promptly responded, "I think that you should go and do that because I would never sell this to you ever…Over my dead body!" The buyer walked off and I stood there looking like a deranged woman. I was very sensitive and protective of my product. It was my baby. Whenever someone did not approve or like it, I would take his or her opinion personally and fire off an arsenal of heated words. Angela and Margie would often have to put out the fires I had started, and after so many of these reactive outbursts, they asked me to leave the trade show booth. "Your negative energy is killing our vibe," they both said; I never tried to do sales again after that.

I learned the importance of knowing what you're good at and what you're not good at. I would explain our products and brand to buyers, and once it was time to make the sale, either Angela or Margie would step in. They could handle the buyers' rejection better than I could; for them it was "the art of negotiation and the thrill of closing the sale." To me, rejection was an attack on my product and brand, and I wasn't having any of that. I stuck to what I knew, which was setting up the display table, decorating our booth, and product placement. I let Margie and Angela do the rest and they were great at it. By the end of 2002, we had 300 accounts totaling $630,000.

In January 2003, Lisa – the notorious buyer from Nordstrom who we previously were unable to convince to buy our products (and who I was afraid of) – gave us our first huge retail break. She finally placed an order for 30,000 pairs of *Tip Toes*, totaling $75,000. This was the biggest order we had as up until then, most of our orders were from specialty boutiques and would average around $500. I called Remington to place the order for the cushions. I was beyond excited and ready to get the ball rolling on this order as it would better position the company financially and the revenue would allow us to create more products. I hung up the phone with Remington and felt confident, ready to build on what looked like a new relationship with Nordstrom, and eager to nail down more new accounts. It felt as if Nordstrom had finally hired me! We continued to vet specialty retailers and chased down existing customers who were delinquent in paying their accounts. We were busy worker bees and with this new account on the table, we felt unstoppable.

In February, with a couple weeks remaining until we received our shipment, I came home after a day of meetings to a stack of letters and bills. While rummaging through, I noticed an envelope from Remington Corporation. I placed the other letters on the counter and proceeded to open the letter. As I read the letter, my mouth dropped in terror and I felt a wave of anxiety and nausea run through me. The factory had produced the cushions but would not ship them. I owed them $150,000 and the company had threatened to halt shipment until I paid them. I started to panic and had to grip the counter to keep my balance. I picked up the phone and called Remington, where I was placed through to their accounting department and begged for an extension on the payment. I knew that if they shipped the cushions, I'd be able to put some money down on the balance as I'd receive payment from Nordstrom in 30 days. The representative didn't budge and wouldn't back down on full payment. I felt the blood rush through my body to my face. I was livid.

Me and Angela

Within seconds, I started cussing out the representative and yelled my frustration at them halting shipment. If we didn't receive the shipment, our business could quite possibly be forced to shut down. I had tapped out Armando who had already invested $250,000 in Foot Petals, and one-third of our customers were late on payment. I continued to yell at the representative until I realized he wasn't going to budge. I couldn't believe that all of our hard work in netting this account was about to go down the drain. I didn't like how it felt to have someone outside of the company determine the fate of our company with a single letter and phone call. I cried and screamed out in desperation. I just knew there was no way of getting out of that situation.

After yelling at the top of my lungs and screaming every profane word I could possibly think of, I did what I normally did when I was upset, or happy for that matter: I called Margie. I didn't give Margie the chance to fully say "hello" before I spewed out what happened. Margie listened then calmly started to offer me some ideas. After I shot down each one, she finally said, "Well Tina, you have to go talk with them." I told her that I did and that they were unrelenting. "No Tina, go to Ohio and talk to them face to face. It's hard to tell someone 'no' to their face," she said. I thought about it for a minute then quickly doubted that a visit would sway their decision. Additionally, I had $300 to my name, which wasn't enough to cover a round trip ticket. I shared my concerns with Margie and she insisted that I go anyway. After five minutes of back and forth,

I finally agreed to go. I maxed out my credit cards and called to ask them to extend my credit. Thankfully, they honored my request and with the few extra hundred dollars, I purchased a red-eye ticket to fly out to Ohio that same night.

> Your love give me such a thrill
> but your love don't pay my bills I need money
> ~ excerpt from *Money* by Barrett Strong

I made it to Akron, Ohio, at 5 a.m. the next day and quickly changed into my suit in the airport bathroom. I picked up the rental car then drove an hour to Wadsworth, Ohio, where the factory was located. I was nervous, but as I approached the city limits, my nerves subsided and I became more assured in what I had to do. Margie had suggested that I offer the factory ownership of the company, and with some thought I agreed. It made sense: if Remington agreed to my proposition, then the production, distribution, and development of our products would be done at their factory. This would allow Margie and me the freedom to focus on sales and product creation, respectively. I arrived at the Remington Corporation a bit haggard with only my vision and my word. I rung the doorbell and was eventually let in by an employee who looked puzzled that I was there. I was escorted to the conference room where the five Remington owners met.

Tina's Tip

Entrepreneurs often want people to invest in their company but do not think big picture in making that happen. Be willing to offer something worthwhile to get something worthwhile.

They each looked confused and were shocked that I was there. I wasted no time telling them my reasons for being there. "I have an offer you cannot refuse," I said in *The Godfather* style as I walked around the table and passed out *Foot Petals* projections to each owner. They looked at the projections as I watched their facial expressions. The CEO looked up. "Ms. Aldatz, my lead accountant and the head of operations tell me you have quite the vocabulary," he said. I stood there and thought back to the conversation I had the day before with the representative. I felt a brief twinge of embarrassment, but kept my composure. "What guarantee do we have that your projections are accurate? That Foot Petals will actually turn a profit?" I took a deep breath then laid all I had on the table. "I have exactly negative $332 to my name. I haven't been paid in six months. I have taken care of three family members, including my father. For the past three weeks, I've lived on beans, rice, and tortillas. Sometimes tequila," I said. "I begged my credit card company for an increase so that I could fly out here on the red-eye. I slept on the plane, dressed in the airport's restroom, and rented the cheapest car I could get. In spite of all this, I believe in my product and myself so much that I stand in front of you at 7:04 a.m. There is nothing that I won't do to make this company a success."

I stood there in silence and stared at the CEO as he tapped his pencil against the table. "Oh and by the way, here are purchase orders for $46,800. Signed," I said. The CEO sat there for a few minutes more. He finally stood and extended his hand. "Tina, you have a new partner," he said. The other four execs stood and shook my hand. I did it! Foot Petals was no longer in jeopardy of shutting down. We filled out the paper work that morning. I had transferred 10 percent of my shares and Armando transferred 45 percent of his shares to the Remington company, giving them 55 percent ownership and controlling interest of *Foot Petals*. Remington would be responsible for manufacturing and distribution of all *Foot Petals* products. Remington would be more inclined to protect our products from knock-offs and other competitors with similar products since they had a direct stake in the company and the sales. We would be protected, at least at the outset, from any copycats. Remington was the No. 1 insoles manufacturer in the world; to have them as a partner meant that other companies who worked with them wouldn't be able to mimic our designs at least for a year or two after the product was already on the market. I left the factory feeling at peace and happy, which was a welcomed change from the frustration and desperation I had felt 24 hours prior. I returned to California with the Nordstrom order on track for shipment, a new partner, and a bottle of tequila.

Don't stop believin'
hold on to that feelin'
~ excerpt from *Don't Stop Believin'* by Journey

Jen, Margie, Me and Susan at our New York City debut

CHAPTER SEVEN
New Landscape

The partnership with Remington placed *Foot Petals* on a fast track to growth and success. I knew going into the meeting what such a collaboration would do for *Foot Petals*, but admittedly I was surprised at how quickly we were able to reap those benefits. The Remington Corporation was a multi-million dollar company run by five men, the good ole boys as I called them, each with experience in being profitable and running businesses. They had infrastructure and systems already in place that we were able to plug into. Before the partnership, we tried to get into big retailers such as Neiman Marcus and Dillard's but were always asked, "Are you EDI compatible?" EDI, electronic data interchange, is a system required by all major retailers that allows the exchange of business documents such as purchase orders and invoices between a buyer's computer and a supplier's computer system.

We were not EDI compatible and additionally did not have the money to register for Universal Price Codes with each major retailer, which they required and was $10,000 per retailer. After the merger, we became EDI compatible and had the money to register for the UPCs. What would have taken us three to five years and a lot of money, we did in one day through the partnership. Our inventory levels became easy to manage and the costs of goods went down.

The Remington partnership also provided me with direct access to an abundance of knowledge these men had in business. I could not have paid for the education I received from these men as it gave me so much power and insight into the way business was done. With controlling interest, Remington was responsible for all tax filings, legal expenses, and trademarks. I had the security of knowing I had money, a factory that wouldn't produce copied products to my competitors, and I locked in the security of knowing my competitors wouldn't be able to knock us off for at least a year. I may have had a smaller piece of the pie, but as I saw it, I'd rather have a smaller piece of a big pie than a big piece of a small pie.

Things were finally on the upswing and I started to feel a bit more stable and secure business wise. My family seemed to be OK. I'd drive by my brother's school when the day was over to watch as my dad picked him up. I wanted to be sure they were all right and figured this was the best way to keep an eye on them while not getting too involved. My Aunt Lonnie kept me in the loop as well and prompted me on many occasions to go see my dad as she was concerned for his safety and wellbeing. With the growth of the company and my increased travel schedule, I didn't have as much time to deal with family issues. My drive-bys had to suffice although I missed my dad and younger siblings terribly. In the midst of everything, I managed to start dating, which was a welcome change.

Randy and I met during a trip to Vegas for a trade show I attended with Margie and Angela. At 6'3", Randy walked into my line of vision while the girls and I were out for dinner at an upscale steakhouse on the Las Vegas Strip. He was tall and stocky with olive-hued skin and resembled actor Benjamin Bratt, which made me swoon even more!. I expressed my interest in him to the girls over cocktails, but didn't plan on making my admiration known beyond our table. Leave it to Angela to up the ante; she dared me to approach Randy, who was sitting with a few other guys, and strike up a conversation. I balked at the challenge but eventually accepted after a couple shots of Tequila helped to calm my nerves.

As I stood up to walk over to his table, Randy stood up and started to walk towards my direction. We stopped a few feet away from each other, in front of the empty table that stood between both parties. I was startled that he started the conversation first. I later discovered that he had been eyeing me the entire time. When he saw me get up, he assumed that I was about to leave and wanted to make a move before it was too late. Smart man. We talked for a few minutes, long enough to exchange courtesies and for me to find out that he lived in southern California as well. He was a fireman and was in Vegas celebrating his best friend's last night as a bachelor. Angela and Margie walked over and joined us as I handed Randy my business card. "Perhaps our office could use a little safety inspection if you know what I mean," Angela said. (She overheard Randy say that he was a fireman.) "You make sure to give my sister a call." The following Monday, Randy came to my office in Culver City and invited me to lunch. We went out and began dating that day.

I was happy. I had met a great guy who I started to fall in love with and had a company that was evolving day by day. About a month or two after the partnership, Remington sent its accounting department and account managers to our office to get under the hood of the company. They stayed at our office for a few weeks and delved into our systems and books to get the business under control. We still had quite a few delinquent accounts and outstanding balances from retailers, and I was pressed by Remington execs to stop selling to them. Some of these retailers included fashionable boutiques that catered to celebrities and I wasn't eager to let them go. The endorsements from their clientele could expose and help promote our brand, which in my mind was good publicity. The delinquent accounts were bad business for *Foot Petals*, which I eventually came to see. In that first year of working with Remington, I had shut down 100 accounts, and the average number of days it took a retailer to pay us went from 120 to 45 days. I had emphasized pushing the product and building a brand so much that I didn't realize I was risking everything by maintaining delinquent accounts. It was tough to go in and cut off relationships that I had prior to the partnership, but I learned that cutting off what didn't work was the only way to grow and reach our fullest potential as a company.

CREATING COMPANY CULTURE

While working on some paperwork, my office manager came in to my office with a confused look on her face. "Um, Tina," she said. "They (Remington people) want some alcohol." I looked up at her and found the request a bit odd, so I asked, "Alcohol? What, rubbing alcohol?" She cleared her throat then whispered, "No, they want a cocktail." I looked at my watch and it wasn't even quite 5 p.m. yet. "What?" I said completely thrown off as it was too early in the day for alcoholic beverages, or so I thought. We discovered that it was customary, a tradition for them

"Margarita Fridays" at Foot Petals office

to drink alcohol around 5 p.m. so I went out and picked up a few bottles of Jack Daniels and other spirits and brought it back to the office. They poured their drinks and went back to work. I had never witnessed anything like that before and thought it was cool. After they left back for Ohio, I borrowed the idea and incorporated "Margarita Fridays" and alcohol at work into our company culture.

We had a small staff and it was important to me that everyone felt included, respected, and appreciated. We worked hard and every woman on staff went above and beyond to ensure that the work of the company was done to the best of her ability. We had a solid team of women who were invested in the company and spoke of it as if it were their own. I was fortunate to be surrounded by people who were not only good at their positions, but were passionate and believed in the company too. And they were patient with me. At the time, there wasn't another company like *Foot Petals* that we could borrow ideas from, so we had to create everything ourselves: job descriptions, job titles, everything. Most of the time, we didn't know what we needed until a situation arose that showed us, "Oh we need that." We all learned and implemented as we went along, which can be hard as everyone loves structure. I was blessed to have people in my corner who understood that what we were doing hadn't been done before and would require that we all stretch outside of our comfort zones. Even my friend Mistala, who by this point no longer worked for ABC, would come out to the office with her newborn baby boy and help us make phone calls and fold boxes for our product.

Our team continued to grow and as it did, I kept at the forefront a commitment to a fun, loving, and liberal work environment where trust was key. I didn't have a timesheet or official time tracking system implemented as I didn't want people to feel locked in to a certain number of set hours each day. I had established that our office hours were from 9 a.m. to 5 p.m. Mondays through Fridays. If it worked out for a staff member to come in at 11 and work until 7, or leave early one day and stay later another, then it was perfectly fine by me. We operated on an honor system and it worked out well for our company. I believed in and provided our staff with an environment that made them want to come to work each day and made sure their benefits and salary packages met their expectations and was commensurate with their experiences. I knew that these women could take their talents to a more established company but they chose to stay with me. This meant the world to me and I made sure they not only knew it, but felt it, too, by how I treated them. We worked hard and played hard and we all made time to fill the other in on what was going on in our personal lives. We knew if one person was going on a date and we celebrated in each other's life moments (i.e. engagements, baby showers, births, and even deaths). These women were not just my staff, they were like my sisters.

Sisters are doing it for themselves
Standing on their own two feet
And ringing their own bells.
Sisters are doing it for themselves!
~ excerpt from *Sisters Are Doing it for Themselves* by Aretha Franklin

Annual Spa Day with the girls. Renee, Susan, Sharol, Jaz, Tina, Angela, Susan, Kristel, Tamara and Aeli

CLOSE TO HOME

I was headed out of town for a business meeting in April 2004 when my Aunt Lonnie called. She was concerned about my dad and had asked that I go check on him. He was getting caught up with the gangs again and she feared his life might be in danger. I assured her that he would be fine and that my dad was just being himself. I told her I would check on him when I got back from my travels, and left for my business trip.

About a week after my business trip, I was back at the office holding a marketing meeting with staff. I was right in the middle of answering a question when my secretary came over and said I had a phone call. I excused myself from the meeting and went into my office where I could take the call. "Hello," I said. "Tina, this is your cousin David…they're saying in the neighborhood that your dad is dead. They killed him…they killed him in front of the laundry mat." I didn't move and couldn't bring my lips to speak a single word. "I need you to go down to the coroner's office on Mission." I sat there, stunned and immobile as the reality and weight of my cousin's words started to sink in. "Please go over there," he said. I hung up with my cousin then closed the door. I felt the tears roll down my face and a lump form in my throat. I screamed and grabbed my stapler then threw it against the wall. I could not believe my father was dead.

FROM STILETTOS TO THE STOCK EXCHANGE

There was no way my father was dead. I sobbed and wailed and felt deep regret. My aunt had feared that my dad's life was in jeopardy and had asked me to go check on him, but I didn't. "Dad, I'm so sorry," I whispered between sobs. No words could describe how hurt and angry I felt at the world and myself at that moment.

> You're my love. You're my angel.
> You're the girl of my dreams.
> ~ excerpt from *Daddy's Home* by Shep and The Limelites

Some of the girls at the office drove me home and called Randy for me. He immediately left work and picked me up from our apartment and together we headed over to the coroner's. Rocky was driving to the coroner's from Laguna, which was about two hours away in traffic. Randy and I arrived first; about an hour later, Rocky pulled up. I was hysterical as I tried to grasp the idea of our father being deceased. Rocky walked towards me and grabbed my arm to help me keep balanced. His eyes were bloodshot red and mirrored my own. We walked in to the L.A. County Department of Coroners and waited in the hallway. Finally the coroner came out into the hall where we were standing. "You have my father…Arturo Aldatz," I said. "I don't think

From left: Rocky, Dad, Tio Bobby, Little David, Tio David

that…," the coroner said before I cut him off. "Where's my dad? Where's my dad?" I questioned. "We are trying to confirm that," he said. I looked through the window and saw a body on the table. There was a toe tag on the left foot that read John Doe. "He's not a John Doe!" I yelled. I kept screaming at the coroner that my dad wasn't a "John Doe" and asked him to let me see my father. I was shaking uncontrollably; I just wanted to see my dad. I explained that my name was tattooed over his heart and my sister's name, Angela, was on the right and a cross was in the middle of his chest. The coroner expressed that he didn't think it was a good idea for me to identify the body, which only made me even more upset. Rocky said he'd go in instead and left me with Randy and my uncle. I watched Rocky walk towards the table. The coroner lifted the cover on the left side just enough for Rocky to see. He nodded his head and the tears started to run down his cheeks. Rocky walked out of the morgue and stared directly into my eyes. I knew at that moment that it was indeed our father lying on that table.

I left the coroner's and went home where I blacked out for a week. I drew the curtains and stayed in my room. I only wanted to retreat into the darkness and be comforted by the silence and my mother. My mom stayed with me that entire week. She never left my side. She took me to the hospital to gather my father's belongings and to sign documents as 'next of kin.' While at the hospital, I saw a chapel and begged my mother – who wasn't religious and hadn't gone to a church since she was 16 years old – to go inside with me so that together, we could pray for my father's soul. She reluctantly agreed to go in with me, and together we prayed while the tears flowed without a sign of ever letting up.

So many thoughts rushed through my mind as I tried to piece together my father's death. I felt sadness, I felt rage, and I felt guilt. My Aunt Lonnie had talked with the woman who owned the laundry mat; she told Aunt Lonnie that my father would park his van there every night. I cried to the point that I thought I had no tears left but somehow more tears would always fall. I couldn't comprehend that my father was dead. Knowing that I couldn't talk with him or see his face pained me deeply.

Since my dad was murdered, the coroner couldn't release his body until a cause of death was determined. I gave the detectives and Los Angeles Police Department some time to investigate the circumstances of his death, but their search yielded no leads. I asked Randy to use his influence as a Fireman to get some answers, but that didn't work either. I realized that they probably wouldn't make my father's case a priority and after two weeks, told them to label my father's death an accident. I understood that labeling it an accident meant the police would no longer investigate the details of his death, and I was OK with that. I just wanted my father's body and as long as the case was open, we wouldn't be able to do that. They ruled his death an 'accident' and signed off on the paperwork so that we could finally get my dad's body.

I left the police department and I received a phone call from someone who said they were a friend of one of my cousins. "I was told to deliver a message to you," the person said. "Don't worry about nothing. We're taking care of it. You got my word." They hung up right after saying that. I was confused and wondered who the person was. I took a deep breath and let out a long sigh. Sometimes the streets had a way of righting the wrong when the law enforcement couldn't. Since my father was part of a gang, the members believed wholeheartedly in taking care of their own; they took it upon themselves to find out what happened and would handle things accordingly. It wasn't the exact way I would've liked things to be handled, but there didn't seem to be any other option.

> Amazing grace, how sweet the sound
> That saved a wretch like me.
> I once was lost, but now I'm found
> Was blind, but now I see.
> ~ excerpt from *Amazing Grace* by John Newton

Me and Eric, our first Christmas together as a permanent family

IN SEARCH OF 'NORMAL'

After my dad's funeral, I slowly started to give my attention back to *Foot Petals*. I found it increasingly hard to focus on anything outside of my desire to have a normal family, and my father's death left me feeling like there was a huge void in my life. I clung to my relationship with Randy as it provided a sense of security and stability that I had desired and that had been missing. I felt protected and with time, started to express my desire to get married and for us to start a family of our own. My youngest brother, Eric, who was 11 years old, came to live with me and Randy after our father's death. He was brought to me after his mother was evicted from another apartment. Kady, who had also been living with her mom, moved to Dallas, Texas, with Angela and her daughter Jaz. Both Kady and Jaz were around the same age so it made more sense for Kady to live with them.

Slowly, our condo in Huntington Harbor turned into a home and I was able to provide some stability for Eric. He had moved around so much in his 11 years from our dad to his mom to me then back again. I was happy to have him with me and was glad that I was in a better financial position to care and provide for him. Although I wasn't his mother, I was able to expose him to a two-person household environment, something that he hadn't experienced since he was three years old. With Randy around, Eric had a dominant and positive male example in his life, and

Angela, me and Rocky

they became close. Randy encouraged Eric to play sports, and would attend all of his games, which only sealed their bond. Towards the end of 2004, Randy proposed and I said, "Yes." I was finally getting my chance at normalcy in my home life and felt that marrying Randy would be the missing piece to the puzzle of my life.

In the summer of 2005, Randy and I wed at the Princeville Resort in Hawaii. We had a small wedding, only 15 attendees, that included both of our families and Armando, who had become like a family member to me. I was so happy and felt fulfilled; being married was what I had always wanted. I knew my family was concerned for me and questioned whether I made the right decision in marrying Randy. They had expressed their concerns before the wedding and were vocal in sharing how they were worried because he consumed alcohol frequently and seemed "sneaky." They said my dad would've been disappointed that I had married a guy he considered a "punk." Before my dad died, I took Randy to see him so they could meet. My dad begged me not to bring Randy the "punk" into our family, but I figured he was just being protective as he had always been with guys I dated. Quite honestly, my father never approved of any of the men I brought home so I knew Randy would be no different. As I danced with Randy at our reception, surrounded by family and the sound of the ocean behind us, nothing else mattered at that moment. Nothing.

Always and forever each moment with you
Is just like a dream to me that somehow came true
And I know tomorrow will still be the same
Cause we've got a life of love
that won't ever change.
~ excerpt from *Always and Forever* by Heatwave

CHAPTER EIGHT

Rebuilding The Reputation

F*oot Petals* had started to make a name for itself in the market and had become a brand that was loved and cherished by celebrities, stylists, fashionistas, and major retailers alike. In the three years following the partnership with Remington, the company grew 300 percent annually, and had started to make "too much money." As a result, the owners and executives were given bonuses that would sometimes range from $50,000 to $125,000 annually. I was amazed at how well the company was doing and grateful that my formative years of struggle to make ends meet to support my dream was finally paying off.

By late 2005, our team outgrew our 750-square foot office and had to relocate to a space that could handle our growth. A good friend of mine had a father who owned a two-story, 2,500-square foot building that was located on Venice Boulevard and La Cienega in Los Angeles. Once I expressed to my friend that we were looking to move into a new space, he connected me with his father, who then agreed to let us rent the entire building from him. On top of that, he gave me complete autonomy and creative control on decorating and sprucing up the space. I hired a company to paint the entire outside of the building pink, and had an interior designer rehab the inside. We installed black and white tile on the floor, and had pink carpet laid out in the office areas. I had a 14-member staff split between three states: Margie had an office in Jersey with two people on her sales team; the Remington office had two staff; and the Los Angeles office had the remaining nine staff members. We maintained our fun and liberal office environment and continued to create and produce new products. By 2006, we had 50 products in over 1,000 retailers, and had started distributing internationally.

Creatively, I was on a roll and it helped that I didn't have to bog down my mind with the day-to-day logistics and details of the company. I am definitely a right-brained person. The smallest things could spark my imagination and I would take the idea and run with it. Take for example the day I was pulled over for speeding. I was on my way home from work when the cop clocked me in at 85 miles per hour in a 55 mph zone. As the officer typed up my ticket, I noticed the gun and handcuffs on his holster. I had seen both items several times on TV but on this particular day, each stood out to me. In the time it took the officer to process my information, I had an idea for what I knew would be an amazing, out-the-box, kick-ass ad campaign. And this time, we actually had the budget to do it! I started to sketch out three concepts for the campaign. The first concept was of a foot hanging from a noose with the words *Shoe-icide is NOT the answer* underneath. The second concept was of a woman's feet in a pair of high heels standing on the ledge of a building with the same tagline. The third concept was of an outline of a woman's legs in heels sketched on the pavement with caution tape around it, similar to a murder scene. I was so excited with the "shoe-icide" campaign and knew that consumers and retailers would love the play on words.

There were so many women who would wear their heels to be sexy even if the pain killed them. I often heard women in my circles say, "These shoes are killing me." I even employed the help of one of the Remington owners on the campaign. I needed a noose and no one I knew in L.A. knew how to tie one. I remembered that he was a Boy Scout troop leader and asked him to make one for me, which he did. When I walked in to the office with the noose, everyone looked at me as if I were crazy and wondered what I was up to. I assured them that it would be "genius" and they would love it once I showed them the full concept. We wrapped the photo shoot for the campaign in one week and the images turned out exactly how I imagined. I had a friend Alex who had billboard space near the Beverly Center in Beverly Hills who would let me use it for a discount whenever he didn't have an ad up. I sent the artwork over to him to place on the billboard. On Dec. 30, 2006, a few days after the ad went up, Iraqi leader Saddam Hussein was hung.

Our ad received attention but it wasn't the attention I initially anticipated. CNN, who was covering Saddam's death and getting public opinion on it, did a segment in front of the building where the billboard stood. They asked pedestrians their views on the billboard considering the recent hanging of Saddam Hussein. Some people thought it was a cool concept and felt the ad was unrelated to his death, which it wasn't. The majority of people interviewed however thought the ad was insensitive and cruel. They couldn't believe that our company would make light of Saddam's death. I was baffled. The ad had nothing to do with Saddam's hanging and had been in

the works a few months prior to his death. Matters only became worse when the Suicide Hotline became involved. They took the ad personally and felt we were taking the implications of suicide lightly. I did my best to keep my frustration at bay. I felt that the ad was clear in saying that "shoe-icide" was **NOT** the answer. We kept the billboard up. A couple weeks later, I received a call from Lisa, the buyer from Nordstrom's requesting that I take the ad down. She had received a letter from the Suicide Hotline who threatened to boycott Nordstrom's stores unless we remove the ad. If we didn't, then she would pull our products from all of their stores. I asked my friend to remove the "shoe-icide" ad from the billboard and we replaced it with an ad of the company logo and our tagline underneath: For women who have a love-hate relationship with their sexy heels. I wrote a public apology letter to the Suicide Hotline and donated a generous sum to the organization.

3R's Core Values: Reputation

Your reputation is one of your most valuable assets and it can either help or hurt you. Your reputation is built on relationships and trust. After our shoe-icide campaign went south, we had to regroup and refocus on how to undo any damage to our reputation the campaign might have caused. We had to shift public perception of the company before we lost the trust we had built with our consumers. It's important to the longevity of your business to consider the name your company has for itself. Is it a brand that is trusted? Does it deliver on its products and services? Is it known for its quality? How can you use your reputation to further grow the company? What do you do if your reputation needs repair?

My "genius" idea wasn't so bright, but many people in the industry loved it and saw where I was going with it. Luckily, after the hoopla from the "shoe-icide" ad died down, we got some positive press. A popular TV show at the time, *The Hills*, panned over the Beverly Hills area and stopped at our billboard for at least five seconds. That spot on the TV brought us the favorable publicity we hoped the "shoe-icide" ad would. As a result, interest in the company increased and our sales did too.

MARKET CHANGES

Towards the end of 2007, the global economy started to spiral downward as a result of the crash of the real estate market, the eventual plunge of the U.S. banking industry, and the automotive industries. The market crashes in the United States affected the economies across the world and a global economic crisis ensued. Every industry was hit and the retail industry was no exception. Consumers started to shift from shopping at high-end retailers to shopping at mass retailers such as Target. We noticed this trend, and created an exclusive line of cushions for Target called Fab Feet. The line started out with two items and grew to include 30 products in all 1,500 stores. By catering to mass retailers, we were able to ride out the economic global crisis and continue to have increased sales. Additionally, we landed Dillard's department stores as a customer. By the end of 2007, our company netted $1.9 million pre-tax, which was a 53 percent increase over 2006 on $9 million in sales, a 70 percent increase. It helped that as a company, we avoided "seasonal goods." Our products remained the same year round and were never marked down. A buyer had declared once that, "You all make doing business with you so easy!" We guaranteed our sales; if our products did not sell after 60 days then we happily refunded the money or swapped out the products that didn't perform well with the ones that did at that particular retailer. The way we saw it, if our products did not do well at a store then we didn't want to be there. We also didn't want to punish a buyer for giving us a chance, so if the products weren't selling we'd take our products back and resell it to another buyer.

3R's Core Value: Resilience

One thing that is guaranteed on the path of entrepreneurship is obstacles and curveballs. How a business handles each one is what separates the good from the great. When your company faces a hardship that potentially threatens its existence, ask yourself the following questions: How do I use this crisis? Where can I find opportunity in this? How can I overcome this challenge? Knowing how to navigate the storms, and seeing the potential in them, will help you weather whatever comes your way. Crisis is part of being an entrepreneur; the good news is that your company doesn't have to be ruined as a result of it.

Me and Margie hosting the Footwear News CEO Summit cocktail party in Florida

We knew the sale didn't end once we shipped our product, and that follow-through helped us develop a loyal following. Speaking of loyal: Lisa, the buyer from Nordstrom, called and informed me that we were being knocked off, again. She was approached by companies with similar products to *Foot Petals* and had informed them that Nordstrom had a strict policy not to undermine their original designers. Lisa had shown her dedication to Nordstrom and our brand, and I've always admired and appreciated her for that. If Nordstrom had an award for commitment to a higher moral and ethical standard, she should have been a recipient of it.

As people's preference in retailers changed, so too, did the way people shopped. Instead of going out to stores to shop, more people started to shop online and via television networks such as Home Shopping Network. Thanks to a chance meeting with HSN executive Mindy Grossman, we developed a partnership with HSN that introduced our brand to a new demographic and increased our sales.

My mama told me, you better shop around
oh yeah, you better shop around.
~ excerpt from *Shop Around* by Smokey Robinson

My wedding day

Tina's Tip

Bottom line: Think like a buyer and remember the sale doesn't end once you ship your product. It's about forming partnerships and building trust with your clients.

Margie and I were at the annual Footwear News CEO Summit, a black-tie event in New York City. *Foot Petals* was one of the sponsors and we had a display set up in the hallway to showcase our brand. We were at our table when the director of the event approached me. She asked if I had a moment and I followed her to the ladies lounge. "Is everything OK?" I asked. "We have a problem," she finally said. "Our keynote speaker cannot go on because she is in terrible pain." We walked inside and on the couch sat a sophisticated, blonde woman in an expensive evening gown rubbing her right foot. "My shoes are literally killing me, I cannot walk on stage," Mindy Grossman said, then handed me her shoes, a brand new pair of Louboutins with the signature red bottom sole. She went on to say that the back of her heels and the balls of her feet were burning. I told her I had a solution then ran out to our booth and plucked a Foot Petals kit. I rushed back into the ladies lounge and placed the cushions into her shoes. I placed the shoes on Mindy's feet and watched as she walked around in them. "They feel like new shoes," she said. "Wow...thank you!" She then asked the director to move Margie and me to her table so that she could get to know us more. By the end of the event, I was invited to present Foot Petals on her channel. The first time on, we sold out all of our products that we had designated for that filming. We were asked back and became regulars on the network. This was also the beginning of a long-lasting friendship with Mindy and her husband, Neil.

In March 2008, *Foot Petals* was named one of the fastest-growing companies in the United States by *Inc* magazine and was profiled by *Forbes* magazine. By our eighth year in business, we had reached $10 million in annual sales. We continued to create new products and had partnered with online shoe retailer Zappos to build Foot Petals' pads into Zappos brand shoes. The growth was rapid and my schedule picked up even more. Between business trips domestically and abroad, trade shows, and other meetings I was hardly ever at home. I noticed the change in my marriage and knew my frequent trips didn't help.

Randy and I made nice salaries but for some reason our accounts had started to come up short. Since I traveled extensively and frequently, we decided Randy would be in charge of balancing and managing our finances. I had trusted him with taking care of our home on the days he wasn't at the fire station and making sure all bills were paid. When I questioned him on why our monthly statements were coming up short, he became defensive and would flip the conversation to where it seemed I was being a nag. Things were so touchy and I wanted us to be happy again. I invited him on my business trips so that we could spend time together, but he would refuse my offers. Randy started to drink heavily and would spend time with his friends even when I was home. The odds of us holding a regular conversation were slim to none. I missed him and longed for stability in our marriage. I became increasingly suspicious of his actions when I wasn't around, but since I didn't have any concrete, tangible evidence, I couldn't prove anything.

The year only grew progressively worse for our marriage. I had discovered that he had taken out a second mortgage on our condo without me realizing what I had signed off on. I trusted him. We got into a huge argument and since it was days before Thanksgiving, I suggested that we both spend time with our families for the holidays. Randy went and stayed with his family, and I invited my family to the condo. I had shared with them the news about the second mortgage and my suspicions that Randy was up to something. Eric had witnessed Randy on the computer a lot and shared with Rocky that he suspected Randy was gambling. When Rocky came over to the house, he went in to the office where Randy's computer was, figured out the password, and logged in. He checked Randy's Internet history. There were lists of online gambling sites he frequented. When Rocky checked his e-mail, we discovered something far more unsettling: Randy was seeing another woman. There was a folder in his e-mail with online receipts of purchases, hotel stays, and restaurant bills for two on days that I wasn't in town. I was hurt, upset, and embarrassed. I had placed so much trust in him and felt foolish for not adhering to the red flags earlier on. I was done and wanted to file for divorce right away. Since it was the holiday, I had to wait until that Monday. I went to my lawyer and filed papers for separation and had the locks on the condo changed. When Randy returned from his trip, he didn't know what hit him.

A week later, I was served with a lawsuit: State of California vs. Tina Aldatz. Randy was suing me for alimony. I couldn't believe what a loser he really was! I tried to remind him that I was his wife and that a real man would've been ashamed to sue his woman to receive financial support. Nonetheless, we went to court and were unable to reach an agreement. My business partners, attorney, and investors wanted me to end the suit as soon as possible, and encouraged me to settle. I made Randy an offer to settle our divorce for six figures and made it clear that it would be the one and only offer I made. I told him I would spend the next 10 years and all the money necessary to guarantee he would not receive one red cent. He saw how serious, and livid, I was and signed the document. I paid him the money to finalize our divorce. Good riddance! It was a crazy situation. Although I didn't do anything wrong, I was hurt, betrayed, and embarrassed. I waited until I was 35 years old to get married because I figured I was older, more mature, and wouldn't have to deal with issues such as the ones Randy and I were in. Our marriage only lasted for three years. Since I did not have a pre-nuptial agreement and we lived in a "no-fault state," I had to agree to accept all debts including the second mortgage and all of the credit card balances that accumulated. So much ran through my mind and I started to feel regret. I wished I had listened to my dad and family when they begged me not to bring him into our family. I wanted to hide. There I was: a successful and smart, 38-year-old woman who was unsuccessful in her love life. I was ashamed and had a 3-day nervous breakdown. A few years later, Randy called and apologized for ruining our marriage. He actually took full responsibility, although he never gave me back one cent of my money. Go figure!

"Figure out who you are separate from your family
and the man or woman you're in a relationship with.
Find who you are in this world and what you need to feel
good alone. I think that's the most important thing in life. Find
a sense of self because with that, you can do anything else."
- Angelina Jolie

CHAPTER NINE

Positioning For Greatness

My divorce knocked the wind out of me and I felt like a rug had been yanked from under my feet. After my nervous breakdown, I took a few days to center myself and get back up to speed as much as possible. I still battled feelings of shame, embarrassment, and deep regret, and knew that those emotions wouldn't disappear overnight. With time and prayer, I was able to slowly release what I had been feeling, and eventually accepted the experience as a lesson needed and a lesson well learned. Besides, with the company continuing to grow at warp speed, I couldn't afford to stay away too long. There was still much work to be done, and I had been thinking a lot about not only my future, but the future of *Foot Petals*.

Around early 2009, we started to notice an increase in the amount of competitors with products similar to or nearly identical to our own. There were a handful of 'designer' insole brands that popped up on the market, such as HUE's Fabulous Feet Collection, that had products and even packaging that resembled *Foot Petals*. It was challenging to watch as competitors unveiled their knock-offs that were clearly inspired by our products. I was agitated yet simultaneously encouraged to stay ahead of my competitors in creating even more stylish, trendy, and original products.

In mid-2009, Dr. Scholl's® – who had up until that point specialized in the bulky gel insoles – gave its insoles a new 'designer-inspired' face lift. The company created its Dr. Scholl's® For Her High Heel insoles and had tapped stylist and host of the TLC show, *What Not to Wear*, Stacy London to be the face of the brand. Needless to say, I was upset once their campaign went live. To start, they marketed their insoles as a product that would help women achieve style and comfort, *Foot Petals* anyone? Secondly, Stacy London looked like she could be related to me. From her skin tone, to the jet black hair, to her age, to her height and stature, Stacy London could very well pass as my sister. I felt the similarities were no coincidence. I was so mad at what I felt was a downright duplication of my brand identity that I wrote the CEO of Dr. Scholl's® a heated letter. I blasted their company for being unauthentic and unoriginal, and suggested that they hire a creative team that actually did some work as opposed to copying brand concepts that were already established. I didn't receive a response back but I felt lighter after getting what I felt off my chest. I knew that as long as we were in business that we would have competitors and knock-offs pop up left and right. I also knew that the quality of our products spoke for itself; no matter how many copycats entered the arena, *Foot Petals* would still be distinguished from the rest. I often thought of brands such as UGG boots during this period of knock-offs. I was comforted in knowing that UGG grew their brand year after year in spite of all of the UGG knock-offs that were on the market, and figured it could work much in the same way for *Foot Petals*. It seemed like having knock-offs worked to their favor and was free advertising for them.

TRADEMARKS, COPYRIGHTS, AND PATENT LEATHER SHOES

The *Forbes* magazine article in 2008 garnered the company a lot of attention from competitors and companies who were interested in acquiring the brand. I had started to reach a point where I wanted the company to continue to grow beyond what we could provide for it. We had made our third move, this time to an office space in Long Beach, California, and were steadily increasing our product lines, sales, and market presence. I knew that in order to take *Foot Petals* to the next level that I would have to consider selling the company. I wasn't looking for a big payday or even to retire early, but wanted to do what I knew was in the best interest of the future of the company.

In late 2008, I received a call from H.H. Brown Shoe Company, a Berkshire Hathaway Company. The company had been following *Foot Petals* and wanted to court us for an acquisition. I was shocked as Berkshire Hathaway was a multinational company run by the stock market guru himself, Warren Buffett. I had no idea that any part of Berkshire Hathaway even knew of our company, so to be courted by them was a major deal. The company wasted no time in showing us how serious they were. We set up a meeting with H.H. Brown and all of the Foot Petals partners to discuss a possible acquisition. I was already sold on the potential deal and needed to get the approval from the Remington executives. The day of our meeting, Margie and I were flown from New York on a private jet along with H.H. Brown execs, to Wadsworth, Ohio, to meet with the Remington team. I was impressed and knew that the acquisition would be a surefire move. We all met at the Remington office, and both Margie and I were ready to start the process of acquisition that day. The Remington execs were not on board to sell and blocked the acquisition talks from progressing with H.H. Brown. *Foot Petals* had become so successful, and profitable, that a sale would put a dent in Remington's pockets. I discovered after that meeting just how much of a cash cow *Foot Petals* had become for the Ohio factory, and learned of the tax breaks and incentives the company was afforded because of *Foot Petals*. I saw that any talks of an acquisition would be met with resistance from our Remington partners, but I was determined to move forward in preparing the company to be sold.

Around March 2009, Margie and I attended a footwear trade show event in New York. While there, we met Greg Tunney, CEO of R.G. Barry Corporation, the parent company of the *Dearfoams* slippers brand. We hit it off instantly and felt that there could be a unique collaboration with their company. Greg invited us to dinner and we met with Gordon Zacks, chairman of R.G. Barry and the son of Florence Zacks Melton, the founder and creator of the *Dearfoams* slipper company. We learned a lot about Gordon's mom, her life, and her vision. I felt a connection to the company already and was amazed at how similar its founding story was to *Foot Petals*'. Florence Zacks Melton discovered a piece of foam in the 1940s and invented the first washable house slipper. I was deeply moved and flattered when Gordon said I reminded him of his mother.

Me boarding Remington's private plane

FROM STILETTOS TO THE STOCK EXCHANGE

An acquisition of *Foot Petals* by R.G. Barry seemed inevitable but there were quite a few loose ends. In the formative years of the company, I had signed a few licensing deals with companies to help grow the brand. As I began to notify the licensees of my plans to sell *Foot Petals*, I was met with lawsuits and a lot of legal backlash that I had to tend to and settle. In addition, the Remington partners were still not willing to sell. Our relationship quickly deteriorated as I saw that they were only concerned with how their pockets would be affected by such a sale. They didn't seem to care about what was in the best interest of the company. Eventually – after close to two years – we reached a point where we all agreed that it was time to sell. I had cleared up the last few stray ends of legal matters that would prevent a sale from going through. *Foot Petals* was ready for the taking.

In December 2010, the R.G. Barry Corporation presented us with an offer for acquisition. The company wanted to purchase *Foot Petals* for $14 million and I would stay on as president and founder of the brand for three years. I believed that R.G. Barry could take *Foot Petals* from a $10 million company to a $50 million company in a short period of time. I also felt that R.G. Barry wasn't so big of a company that *Foot Petals* would get lost in it and/or overshadowed. I knew that my baby would be in good hands from the moment Margie and I met with Gordon and Greg two years earlier. On January 28, 2011, I accepted the offer for R.G. Barry to acquire *Foot Petals* and sold the company only a decade after its founding.

I'll be seeing you
In all the old familiar places
That this heart of mine embraces
All day through and through
I'll find you in the morning sun
And when the night is new
I'll be looking at the moon
But I'll be seeing you.

~ excerpt from *I'll Be Seeing You* by Billie Holiday

I stayed in a daze for at least three months before it finally sunk in that I had sold *Foot Petals* and was a newly minted multimillionaire. I was filled with so many emotions such as joy, peace, sheer excitement, curiosity, relief, and gratitude that on most days it was challenging to contain it all. My entire life I had worked to provide for my family and had stretched myself out of my comfort zone to ensure that my family didn't go without the basic necessities. I had struggled so much earlier on that I felt fortunate to finally be able to give and provide for them without lack or limitation. I established college funds for each of my younger siblings, niece, and nephews, and had purchased cars for my mom and siblings. I missed my dad and wished that he could have been there with us to celebrate as I knew he would've been proud of my accomplishments. I could almost hear him cheering me on with pride saying, "Oh mija, you did it!"

A month after the acquisition, I flew to New York to witness *Foot Petals* being exchanged on the stock market. The wind was sharp and pierced with a vengeance through my winter white wool coat. I stood on the curb and waited for my driver, George, to come pick me up from the airport. George had been Margie and my driver since 2001 when we first created *Foot Petals*. He would always pick us up from the airport and see to it that we made it to all of our appointments and destinations. He was a part of the *Foot Petals* family, and was always one of the first people to know the results of a meeting.

As the black Lincoln Town Car pulled up, I smiled when George came around to open my door. Once in the car, I shared with him that we had sold the company and that I wanted to stop by Wall Street to observe the company being traded for the first time before heading to our new showroom. I described in great length the details of signing day and watched in the mirror as George's eyes watered. If there was anyone who had gone through the trenches with us, it was George. He knew our battle stories and could write just as detailed a book as we could on our *Foot Petals* adventures. We reminisced on some of our fondest memories and laughed as we both recalled the meeting Margie and I had in Texas with Alex Dillard, president of Dillard's department stores. We had a proposal that would place our products in all of the Dillard's stores. The deal would bring in millions to the company, and we were naturally stressed and a bit anxious as to how it would turn out. Minutes prior to the meeting, I had to use the bathroom and told Margie my situation. She urged me to "hurry up" as the Dillard's team would be there any minute. I rushed to the bathroom and hurriedly started walking back towards our showroom. I noticed that the Dillard's entourage was approaching so I picked up speed.

I had prepared for the meeting by buying a tan Diane von Furstenberg dress, with tan Donna Karan fishnet stockings, and a pair of tan patent leather pumps. As I walked briskly towards the showroom, my patent leather shoes stuck to each other and I fell – knees and hands first – to the ground. I was walking so fast that when I fell, I had burned a hole at the knees in my stockings and had torn the skin from the palms of my hands. I limped back into the showroom and attempted to explain to Margie what happened, but I was out of breath. She was able to make out what happened and rearranged the set-up of the tables and chairs so that I could sit the entire presentation. The Dillard's team walked in; after they sat down, I dove into our presentation. I remained seated the whole time and none of the Dillard's team seemed to notice. We closed the deal and as soon as they walked out, we went to the ladies room so that I could clean myself up. We went out for cocktails immediately afterwards.

George and I laughed as we recalled the details of that day, and other moments that he had experienced with us. As we approached Wall Street, I pulled out a folded piece of paper from my pocket. When I was in the third or fourth grade, I drew a picture of myself dressed in a business suit with a briefcase in my hand. The New York skyline was behind me and I was getting into a black Lincoln Town Car. Even as a little girl I had dreams of one day becoming a businesswoman. I handed the piece of paper to George then looked outside the window at the city's skyscrapers. George got out of the car then proceeded to open my door. I stood up and hugged George as he helped me on to the sidewalk. He placed the drawing in my hand as I watched a flock of school kids in uniforms walk toward the New York Stock Exchange on a field trip. I looked at the drawing, then at the school kids, and then peered up towards the NYSE. I folded the drawing and placed it back in my pocket. I walked towards the NYSE entrance and prepared to walk in to witness *Foot Petals* exchanged on the stock market. I took a deep breath, clutched the drawing in my pocket, and smiled. *Dreams do come true.*

Me and Greg Tunney at HSN's vendor ball

Speaking at the annual Score event about mentoring

EPILOGUE

It's 11 p.m. and I have just walked in to my Laguna Hills home after an eight-hour flight from D.C. I was invited to the Nation's Capital by the Republican National Committee to prep for upcoming debates on immigration as a first-time co-producer for a major motion picture *Frontera*, a film on immigration and human rights. Had it not been for my paternal grandmother, Josephina Diaz, who migrated to the United States in the 1920s, I would not be here today living the American Dream, against all odds. I must say that I do feel that overcoming obstacles is part of my DNA.

My two dogs, Cisco and Diego, greet me at the door as I set my bags and belongings down. I smile because there's no place like home. I turn on the lights and quickly check each room. Eric is asleep. I kiss him on the forehead. He always comes home from UCLA for the weekend even though he has his own apartment. Shortly after selling *Foot Petals*, I bought this house, known as "The Hub," for my family. I wanted to have a central location where we could all gather and live together, a safe haven that could never be taken away.

Equally important as buying "The Hub" was buying a house in Orange County. I felt, and still feel, an indebtedness and obligation to reside in and give back to this area. Moving to Orange County after my feet were burned opened my eyes and exposed me to a new environment that I didn't know existed before moving. Although the circumstances that caused my family to relocate to Orange County weren't the best, being in Orange County helped me realize and see that we deserved the best and had a chance at having the best. I was exposed to opportunities and lifestyles that made me strive to want to accomplish and achieve great things. As far as I can tell, Orange County is my permanent place of residence. I'm happy with what I refer to as "Tina's Town," this big house with my two dogs, and a constantly revolving door. I'm grateful that my family will always have a place to come to, a place they can call home.

As I take a seat behind my desk, I look at the *Foot Petals* awards and event photos lined strategically along the walls. I stepped down as President of *Foot Petals* after the first year of acquisition (2012), cutting short my contract. I had a hard time dealing with the new corporate infrastructure, the red tape that comes along with that type of structure, and having to report to someone. I was used to calling the shots, which changed drastically after the acquisition. I felt it was in the best interest of the company, and my sanity, that I stepped down. I have come to realize that I am a serial entrepreneur. I didn't suspect at the time that I would experience such emotions as shock and depression, as I still was in disbelief that I sold my company. So much of my identity was intertwined with *Foot Petals* that once I sold it, I immediately felt regret. I felt like I had sold a part of myself. I shared these thoughts with my mother and, as was her nature, she helped me put everything into perspective. "I feel like I sold my child," I told my mother during one of our many conversations that year. "Oh God," she jokingly replied. "Believe me, if somebody would've offered me millions of dollars for one of you kids, I definitely would've taken the deal. Get over it!"

My mom had a way of helping me get out of my head through her humor and just by being her self. I had already come to realize that Fifi was better at being a friend than a mother, but I am thankful that in the last year of her life, I was able to experience her as both. Fifi was my mother's nickname. Once Angela gave birth to her daughter Jaz, my mom refused to be called 'grandma' so she requested that her grandchildren call her "Fifi" instead. The name stuck and everyone started calling her that. After years of alcohol and substance abuse, my mother had developed complications that affected her kidneys and liver. Her health started to decline rapidly towards the end of 2011, and she was frequently in and out of the hospital. We spent a lot of time together, started going to church together, and shared in rituals such as dinner and karaoke in Huntington Harbor that only strengthened our relationship. Those memories overshadow a lot of the bad times we experienced earlier on in our lives and I'm grateful to have had the chance to create new and better memories with her. In February 2012, at 63, my mother made her transition with her family and closest friends by her bedside, smoking weed and watching *The Big Lebowski*, laughing all the while.

After my mom's death, I took some time to figure out next steps and what I wanted for my life. I had reached a place where I felt I was ready to start giving back, and made the decision to commit to my community. I strongly believe that a person should take care of themselves first, their families second, and their community last. If someone has not taken care of his/her self first and are not on as much of a solid ground as he/she can be, then there's no way he/she can give back to their family or community in a truly meaningful way. I became a board member for Girls Incorporated of Orange County where I served on the Board of Directors for two years, 2011-2013, and was invited by the Hispanic 100 to become a board member and to create a mentorship program. I was invited to become Chairwoman of the Hispanic 100 Foundation's Mentorship Program.

Co-Chairing the 2014 Hispanic 100 Foundation's annual gala in Newport Beach

I believe that to whom much has been given, much is required, and I allow this sense of responsibility to be my motivation in all that I do and am doing. I visit foster homes, domestic violence centers, and speak with politicians, community leaders, and economic developers to help entrepreneurs, students, children, and graduates with the hope that something that I say will inspire them to achieve their dreams no matter what obstacles they may have to overcome. I really hope that through speaking engagements – and now this book – that I can share what I have learned from my mentor, Armando DuPont, on the six business essentials 3M's (best practices): *Money*, *Marketing* and *Management* and the 3R's (my core values): *Reputation*, *Resourcefulness*, *Resilience* while encouraging people that they too can have and live the American dream.

I am embarking on a new chapter with my business partner and best friend, Margie, through our company, Savvy Traveler LLC. We are creating a new collection of products to sell globally that will help make the lives of frequent travelers a bit easier. I am even more excited as Margie and her family have moved to southern California, which means we are finally doing business together on the same coast. Margie and I are often referred to as Lucy and Ethel from the popular

1960s sitcom "I Love Lucy" and now with us both on the same time zone, I'm certain that there will be new adventures to be had and new stories waiting to be shared.

I am thankful, truly grateful that God has blessed, and continues to bless the path that I'm on. Admittedly, I have had moments where I felt envious and a bit resentful; I have wished that I didn't work so that I could focus on remarrying and becoming a mother. I have even dreamed of being a housewife. I am sad sometimes that I've never had a child of my own or have been particularly lucky in love, although I do still believe in marriage. I've come to realize that God has blessed me with children in a different way by giving me the ability to be a mother figure to my siblings. In some small way, I am a mother figure to the young adults that I mentor and have employed over the years. I feel God's hand is on my work when I see their faces light up during a conversation, when I see their successes, and hear of their achievements. My heart is very full and my life is rich. Now that my siblings are all grown up, I feel that it is now my turn to focus on myself. I have entered yet another new season, a new chapter in my life and I'm ready to take on each new challenge as it comes. I am a woman on a mission…a serial entrepreneur with a business to run and several more waiting to be born.

Hi Tina,

I read your story and must admit I was floored! You certainly have bared your life and soul on every page; brave indeed. You and Margie and have been terrific. From our first meeting, I knew you both were winners. As a team, you and Margie have such an endearing quality.

You can be proud and rightfully so.
Be proud first as a person and second as a self-made woman.
There are a couple of wise sayings that you embody:

- He/ She who blesses G-d in adversity will have his or her prosperity doubled.

- There is nothing truly valuable which can be purchased without pains and labor.

- We cannot go through life without receiving many arrows that prick and pierce, but there is no need to leave them sticking in us.

I am proud of you, young lady, and I'm glad to be your friend. It is not given to all to command success; we can do more - merit it – and you sure have merited it!

Love you,

Sonny Shar
Chairman, Pentland Group

Tina,

I read your book yesterday afternoon on the flight back from Dublin.

Truly, I'm at a loss for words.
First, I want to let you know how appreciative I am that you shared your life story with me. Thank you.

Second, I've got to say you are remarkable to have found your way through the emotional chaos, hard-knocks, family turmoil and business building in the smoke of 9.11, followed by a global recession and other events. My heart and admiration goes out to you.

And third, what a distinct pleasure and honor it would be for us to work with you on your book launch with a view toward helping strengthen and grow WIFI as a resource for women in the footwear industry. Your story is both harrowing and inspiring. You don't need me to say that to you because you already know. But what you did, how you displayed an extraordinary level of dedication to your family and your business, and how much your life story is a story that women across our industry will understand and need to hear on a deeply personal level, should be cherished. You should also be cherished for being willing to put yourself out there and talk about it. So thank you again Tina.

When can we chat again to move things forward.

All the best,

Neal Newman
President
Two Ten Footwear Foundation

"Difficult, picky, kinda rude" was the way they described her.

But the first time I saw Tina walking through the plaza where I worked, seeing her tap dance over the brick bridge in a yellow dress and killer shoes, I couldn't even care what my coworkers were saying about her. Anyone who is described that way before they even take a step through the door usually means they are someone with a purpose.

I never took my eyes off of her – I was somehow enamored with how stoic, how poised and elegant she was – and the moment she walked in and brought her head up to say hello, I immediately felt a kind of kinship with her.

"Hello, good afternoon" she said to me with rouged lips and a sunlit smile.

I immediately noticed how beautiful she was. Not traditional all-American, more like Veronica Lake meets Snow White.

She started to walk around the counter, and I kept watching her. How could my coworkers not like this woman?

I felt my coworkers behind me rolling their eyes as I approached Tina.

"Hi, how are you?"

She starts to quickly chatter, something about her being on TV she was leaving immediately, needed some jewelry to match her dress and so on. She was nervous and precise all at the same time. She was a woman who knew what she wanted even down to the smallest detail.

I knew I could help her better if I knew how she wanted to feel. She explained she wanted to be vibrant, strong and have a piece that took the sallow out of her skin. Just by looking at her, I knew she craved something that would pop. I showed her a piece, her eyes lit up, she wrapped the necklace around her neck and exclaimed, "That's perfect!"

The other girls came back, surprised I liked her and could find something for her, I shrugged my shoulders, "I dunno, she's not all that bad. It's easy to help her, I get the vision she's going for."

And I did get it. Our lives kept intertwining and eventually I worked for her at Foot Petals. From that first day to present time, Tina Aldatz has had a vision I can see, which I love helping to execute, even if it is just starts with a necklace.

Fatima Jaafari

*this story accounts the writer's first time meeting her future boss and friend, Tina Aldatz. Fatima went on to become one of Tina's personal stylists and then, eventually, an employee at *Foot Petals*.

LYRICAL MUSIC CREDITS AND COPYRIGHT INFORMATION

THEME FROM "NEW YORK, NEW YORK"
Music by JOHN KANDER Words by FRED EBB
© 1977 (Renewed) UNITED ARTISTS CORPORATION
All Rights Controlled and Administered by EMI UNART CATALOG INC. (Publishing)
and ALFRED MUSIC (Print) All Rights Reserved

THE WAY YOU MAKE ME FEEL
Written By Michael Jackson
© 1987 MIJAC Music. All rights administered by Sony/ATV Music Publishing LLC.
All rights reserved. Used by permission.

PAPA WAS A ROLLIN' STONE
Written by Barrett Strong & Norman Whitfield
© 1972 Stone Diamond Music Corp. All rights administered by Sony/ATV Music
Publishing LLC. All rights reserved. Used by permission.

SEASONS CHANGE
Written by Lewis A Martinee
© 1987 Screen Gems – EMI Music Inc. & LNE Publishing. All rights administered by Sony/ATV
Music Publishing LLC., 424 Church Street, Suite 1200, Nashville, TN 37219.
All rights reserved. Used by permission.

I'LL BE THERE
Written by Berry Gordy Jr., Bob West, Hal Davis, & Willie Hutch
© 1970 Jobete Music Co. Inc. All rights administered by Sony/ATV Music Publishing LLC. All rights
reserved. Used by permission

KISS AND SAY GOODBYE
Written by Winfred Lovett
©1970 EMI Blackwood Music Inc. & Nattahnam Music. All rights administered by Sony/ATV
Music Publishing LLC. All rights reserved. Used by permission.

"MR. BIG STUFF"
by Ralph Williams, Joseph Broussard and Carrol Washington
Copyright © 1971 by Peermusic III, Ltd., Malaco Music Co., Caraljo Music
Peermusic III, Ltd. administers on behalf of itself and Malaco Music Co., and Caraljo Music.
Copyright Renewed. Used by Permission. All Rights Reserved

A PLACE IN THE SUN
Written by Bryan Wells & Ronald N. Miller
© 1966 Jobete Music Co. Inc. & Stone Diamond Corp. All rights administered by Sony/ATV Music
Publishing LLC. Used by permission.

THIN LINE BETWEEN LOVE AND HATE
Words and Music by Richard Poindexter,
Robert Eugene Poindexter and Jackie Members
© 1971 (Renewed) Cotillion Music Inc. All Rights Reserved

WE ARE FAMILY
Words And Music By Bernard Edwards And Nile Rodgers
© 1979 Bernard's Other Music (Bmi) and Sony/Atv Music Publishing LLC (Ascap) All Rights For
Bernard's Other Music Administered by Warner-Tamerlane Publishing Corp. (Bmi) All Rights For
Sony/ATV Music Publishing LLC (Ascap) Administered By Sony/ATV Music Publishing Llc All Rights
Reserved

SPINNING WHEEL
Written by David Clayton-Thomas
© 1968 EMI Blackwood Music Inc. & Bay Music Ltd. All rights administered by Sony/ATV Music
Publishing LLC. All rights reserved. Used by permission.

SHE'S GOT HER TICKET
Written by Tracy L. Chapman
© 1988 EMI April Music Inc. & Purple Rabbit Music. All rights on behalf of EMI April Music Inc.
administered by Sony/ATV Music Publishing LLC. All rights reserved. Used by permission.

YOU'VE GOT A FRIEND
Written by Carole King
© 1971 Colgems – EMI Music Inc. All rights administered by Sony/ATV Music Publishing LLC. All
rights reserved. Used by permission.

FOR THE LOVE OF MONEY
Written By Anthony Jackson, Kenneth Gamble & Leon Huff
© 1973 MIJAC Music, Warner-Tamerlane Publishing Corp. All rights on behalf of MIJAC Music
administered by Sony/ATV . All rights reserved. Used by permission.

WORK TO DO
Written by O'Kelly Isley, Ronald Isley, & Rudolph Isley
© 1989 EMI April Music Inc. & Bovina Music Inc. All rights administered by Sony/ATV Music
Publishing LLC. All rights reserved. Used by permission.

"DON'T STOP BELIEVIN'"
Written by Neal Schon, Jonathan Cain, and Steve Perry
Published by Weed High Nightmare Music (BMI)
Administered by Wixen Music Publishing, Inc.

LYRICAL MUSIC CREDITS AND COPYRIGHT INFORMATION

DADDY'S HOME
By James Sheppard and William Miller
Copyright © 1956 (Renewed) by Three Wise Boys Music and © 1961 EMI Longitude Music.
Administered by Sony/ATV Music Publishing LLC. International Copyright Secured. All Rights
Reserved. Reprinted By Permission.

SHOP AROUND
Written by Berry Gordy Jr. & Smokey Robinson
© 1960 Jobete Music Co. Inc. All rights administered by Sony/ATV Music Publishing LLC. All rights
reserved. Used by permission.

ALWAYS AND FOREVER
Words and Music by Rod Temperton
Copyright (c) 1976 RODSONGS Copyright Renewed
All Rights Administered by ALMO MUSIC CORP.
All Rights Reserved Used by Permission Reprinted with Permission of Hal Leonard Corporation

DEJA VU
Lyrics by Adrienne Anderson, Music by Isaac Hayes
Copyright (c) 1979 by Rightsong Music Inc. and Universal Music - Careers
International Copyright Secured All Rights Reserved Reprinted with Permission of Hal Leonard
Corporation

DREAM ON
Words and Music by Steven Tyler
Copyright (c) 1973; Renewed 2001 Music Of Stage Three (BMI)
Worldwide Rights Administered by Stage Three Music (US) Inc., a BMG Chrysalis company
International Copyright Secured All Rights Reserved Reprinted with Permission of Hal Leonard
Corporation

I'LL BE SEEING YOU
from RIGHT THIS WAY
Written by Irving Kahal and Sammy Fain
(c) 1938 (Renewed 1966, 1994, 2006) BMG GOLD SONGS (ASCAP)/Administered by BMG RIGHTS
MANAGEMENT (US) LLC and FAIN MUSIC CO.
All Rights in Canada Administered by REDWOOD MUSIC LTD. and WILLIAMSON MUSIC, a
Division of Rodgers & Hammerstein: an Imagem Company
All Rights Reserved Used by Permission Reprinted with Permission of Hal Leonard Corporation

LYRICAL MUSIC CREDITS AND COPYRIGHT INFORMATION

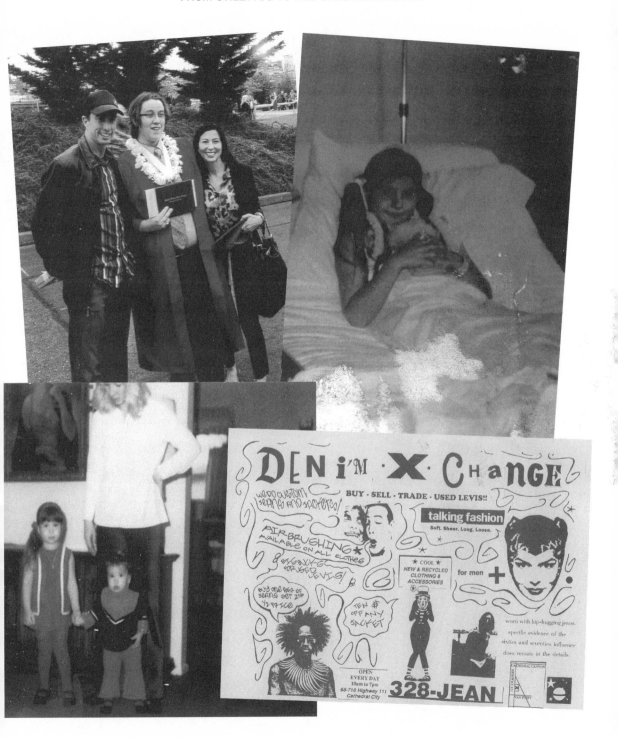

Please join me at
www.TinaAldatz.com

Sign up to receive
exclusive beauty and
travel tips, discounts
and VIP offers before
anyone else!

TINA
ALDATZ

ST SAVVY TRAVELER
SMART · SIMPLE · SAFE

foot petals
wear the shoes you love!